VISHNU PURAN

CW01496965

B. K. Chaturvedi

DIAMOND BOOKS

© Author

ISBN : 81-7182-673-3

Publisher	:	**Diamond Pocket Books (P) Ltd.**
		X-30, Okhla Industrial Area, Phase-II
		New Delhi-110020
Phone	:	011-41611861
Fax	:	011-41611866
E-mail	:	sales@diamondpublication.com
Website	:	www.diamondpublication.com
Edition	:	2006
Price	:	95.00
Printer	:	Aadarsh Printers,
		Navin Shahdara, Delhi- 32

Vishnu Purana   Rs. 95/-

By : B.K. Chaturvedi

Introduction

THE Vishnu Purana is believed to be one of the most important Puranas if not the, most valuable ancient records of the faith called 'Sanatan Dharma' which erroneously often called the Hindu Dharma. It has its value enhanced for two reasons; one, it has detailed description of how a man should live in the world. Secondly, since its base is devotion to Vishnu who is held to be the most important deity of this faith it gathers added significance. Its stories reveal about the various exploits of Vishnu in his different incarnations. But surprisingly it omits certain important incarnation of Vishnu viz. Rana incarnation and the earlier incarnations. It chiefly centres around the incarnation of Vishnu as Lord Krishna, the most potent one all the incarnations of this deity.

In rendering this holy text into English the attention has been paid to cull only those details that are having certain fundamental truths of life. Hence in this work those details have been deliberately omitted which may appear rather confusing or uninteresting to the reader not having the initiation in the sacred lore. The main thrust of the attempt has been to show at least a clear glimpse of our ancient hermitage. No attempt has been made to vary from the text but at places, in order to make the content more unambiguous certain details from other sources like the Mahabharata have been added. It is hoped that those who value our cultural hermitage will accord it a warm welcome. Lastly I express my gratitude to Narendra ji of Diamond Publications for giving me this opportunity.

– B. K. Chaturvedi

Publisher's Note

Puranas are almost like an encyclopaedia listing the human achievements in this part of the world till the time they were edited or compiled. In every cycle of time the master editor called Vedavyas emerges to edit, vet and compile these records. Their significance in enormous even in the present, as they give a peep into the race's distant past of Hindus when the world was evolving and the psyche of the race was being formed. These Puranas record the arguments that make us to decide as to what is hole and what is vile; what is good and what is bad. By going through them we can compare our present -day jurisprudence vis-a-vis the ancient norms. Apart from that, they are a huge store-house of information conceiving every subject under the sun. It is with the view of unearthing these glooms that the present strives of the puranas has been planned.

Contents

Preface

'PURANAS' literally mean ancient or old records. They are almost like an encyclopaediae listing the human achievement in this part of the world till the time they were edited or compiled. In every cycle of time (explained ahead) these occurs a Vedavyas who edits, vets, compiles and even writes these, Puranas with unbiased objectivity. Everyone is not entitled to do this job. Vedavyas is supposed to be the most learned, experienced and awakened person of his cycle to do this job. Vedavyas is a position to which a person is appointed by the learned and pious persons assembly in each cycle. It literally means the one who has fully mastered the Vedas and his position is graphically described as the one who has fathomed the Veda-knowledge as the diameter (Vyas in Sanskrit) does to a circle. In this Vishnu Purana itself the last Vedavyas has himself said that the next Vedavyas would be Ashwatthama of the Mahabharat fame. We know from the Mahabharat that this son of Guru Dronacharya is immortal, though immortality is actually a part of the curse that he has to suffer. In fact Krishna had never cursed anyone in his entire stay on the earth. He cursed Ashwatthama alone. He was made immortal to suffer the pain and humiliation for his oozing filthy wounds right in the forehead. And we know that he was cursed because despite being a Brahman who is supposed to be learned and kind hearted he had asked his Brahmastra (in modern context a deadly nuclear headed missile) to fall on a pregnant lady's: womb so that would be born person's whole lineage could be effaced. This meanness of Ashwatthama appeared so henious to Krishna that he said: "You would see Parikshit (the person who was in the embryo form) ruling over the world from Hastinapur (which roaring about like an unwanted existence all over the world, missing your foul smelling and never healing wounds on the forehead created by the extraction of the gem of congenitally embedded these, you will survive immortally."

What is amazing that the Vedavyas who had created the tome of Mahabharat for the posterity's 'immense brought know will what type of person Ashwatthama had been. How could be suggest his name for such an august past which he himself disenities as above-board? The person holding it cannot be prejudicial or else he would distant the history. The Puranas are like the 'Time-Capsules' left for posterity. No civilization would like to hoodwink its future by deliberately disturbed history. They were not like Macaulay or the like! Perhaps the Vedavyas suggested Ashwatthama's, name for two reasons. first, he is immortal and naturally he would witness all that transpires. Secondly, with time purgating his all mortal confusion and prejudices he is, in the estimation of the last Vedavyas likely to emerge as an impartial observer.

This point has been emphasized to bring home the importance of these Puranas. Normally there are eighteen of these Puranas in a definite order (explained ahead) but some scholar add a few more or replace a few with different names also. Take for example this Vishnu Purana which is also known as Narada-Vishnu Purana[1] in which there are many interproducers. Or many this Purana, The Vishnu Purana, is a pruned version of Narada-Vishnu Purana ! Similarly there is also a 'Skanda' Purana (different from the well known Skanda Puranas). It claimed by some scholars that the famous 'Katha of Bhagwan (god) Satyanarain' Which is recited after completion of every important ceremony like marriage etc in the traditional Hindu Household has been taken from 'this Skanda, Purana'. May be that is time. But the point here is that these Puranas have a definite style of narration and recording the facts. There is invariably one speaker and one listener and their conversation reveals about the importance of one particular deity to whom that Purana is dedicated. Our distinct trend is glomming that deity which breathing the other. This Vishnu Purana in a couple of stories try to lesson the importance of Shiva before Vishnu's Krishna incarnations. This trend had given rise to a kind of violent confrontation between the Vaishnavas and Shaiva in 14th-15th century. Thanks to Tulasidas' Valiant effort the bitterness between the two rests considerably was lessoned.

---

[1] May be the two Puranas were combined for convenience.

Nevertheless, the Puranas are very much part of our sacred love. What is amazing is the values of life that we enrich now are the result of the moral imparted by these stories. Since in the absence of the print or electronic Media these Puranas' recitations was the most effective instrument to influence the masses their impact was naturally paramount. Most of these Puranas, besides giving details about life led about a millennia back, do give us the useful information. In the older times the most powerful king of the Aryavarta used to have them edited and vetted. It is said the last one to get it done was Chandra Gupta Vikramaditya (since 600 A.D.) Since then they are surviving unedited. Anyway for our readership we have edited Vishnu Purana considerably only for making its tales more lucid and relevant.

'The Vishnu Purana' is the first flower of our this garland of 18 more flowers. This series is meant for those that have love for culture but his knowledge of the languages our sacred love has been compile in.

– Publisher

Creation, Sustenance and Dissolution

Discerning the story desire of the curious sages, Suta ji started the narration of the story: 'Following the morning rituals ensuring cleanliness of the body Sage Maitreya reached before the exalted saint Parashar and bowing to him recreationally, he said: 'O Gurudeva! Having completed my education in all Indian scriptured love inducting the Vedas and their Commentaries by your noble grace now I get recognition even from my fellow rivals. But I am still not clear about the following queries:

a. What are the causes that led to the creation of this whole universe? That is, how it came into being and what it shall be dissolving itself ultimately in at the time of final dissolution or Pralaya.

b. What is the mystery behind the creation of this whole earth, it oceans and mountains and the gods that are adorned in it? What limits the sky? What is the basis upon which the earth stands? What provides prop to the sun and other heavenly bodies and what is the scale of this measure?

c. How the divinities came into existence? How was time divided into various Yugas and Manvantras. What decides the occurrence of the final dissolution and who ordains various duties to various beings?

d. What has been the individual achievements of various royal

13

sages (Rajarshis) and Devashis (divine sages) to warrant their names carry much epithets?

e. What is the basis of the classifications made by Sage Vedavyas for human existence and how did he categorise the Vedic texts?

Said Sage Parashar: "Thanks for asking these questions that reminds me of an anecdote connected with Sage Vashistha. As a matter of fact the Puranas themselves are the most authentic source to get answer to these queries. But I tell you something about my personal experience in this context. I learnt once that under the influence of Vishwamitra, a demon had tried to swallow my grand father Sage Vashistha. Charged with vengeance I decided to hold a secrifice with an intention of causing the elimination of the demon race. While the venture was only half-way through Sage Vashistha learnt about my frenzie intentions and he quickly rushed to me to advise:" My son! Anger and Vengeance hamper human development; they destroy the merit in this world and dissipate its balance in the next. Remember it that no one can kill any one. nor can anyone check one's getting one's destiny which get determined by the deeds you do. So the demons will face their fate as destined. Why must you attempt expedite this process at the expense of your merit in both the worlds?

Heeding to my grand pa's advice I stopped the sacrifice. The sage was supremely delighted. It was then that another psychic progeny of Brahma, Sage Pulastya happened to reach there. Grateful at the termination of a venture commenced to cause the elimination of the demon race, his progeny, he blessed me to compile a Purana. This time your asking me questions about the Supreme Being and His Creation made me recollect that boon from the sage now listen to the answer to the questions you raised.

Lord Vishnu is the prime cause of this creation. It is He who materialises it, sustains it and dissolves it, Essential in this whole Universe is manifestation of Lord Vishnu. It is He who in the three different forms. Brahma, His ownself and Shiva causes its creation sustenance and dissolution. What inspire Supreme lord to manifest Himself in myriad forms was only the essence of the discourse that Daksha and other sages gave to king Purukutsu on the banks of the

14

river Narmada He said: Supreme Being is Supreme Lord Vishnu and all the expressed and unexpressed existences emanate from him only. It he who is time that is reckoned between creation and Dissolution. The three characteristics of the creation: Essential (Sattvic), Passionate (Rajasik) and Dull (Tamasik) and the five Basic Elements: earth, air, fire, water and space owe their origin to him only. So is the root of all preparations and sensitivities.

In the beginning of the creation the universe was full of water. In that water first emerged a huge egg which was round like a water-bubble. The egg kept on growing and it had Lord Supreme that is Vishnu inside it. This egg was called Brahmanda. And inside the Brahmanda there were mountains and the land, the oceans and the seas, the gods and the demons in the seed-form. On all sides the egg was covered by water and other basic elements. Inside the egg Vishnu adopted the form of Brahma who proceeded to create the Universe, who creates, who sustains and who dissolves it eventually has already been explained. It is this supreme trinity (Brahma, Vishnu and Mahesh) that is responsible for the three fundamental functions. So salute to Lord Vishnu who is the root cause of all that exists.

There are four Yugas or Epochs. These are called Krita' (or Satya), Treta, Dwapar and Kali and they occur in that order. One Krita Yuga is equal to 4,800 divine years; one Treta to 3,600 divine years, one Dwapar 2400 divine years and one Kaliyug to 1200 divine years. This whole period of time is said to be of 12,000 years[1]. And when all the four epochs or eras (yugas) have completed their 1000 cycles, that is merely one day for Brahma.

One year of mortals is equal to one day of the divine years. As 360[2] is taken as the number of days in the year.

[The whole time division may be better understand by the following equations:]

---

[1] Some version of the Purana claim that Krita has 4000, Treta 3000, Dwapar 2000 and Kaliyug 1000 divine years and thus the whole span of time equals to 10,000 divine years.

[2] The whole time concept of the Hindu being is dominated by the sectors or angles in a circle. As we all know, a circle comprises of 360° hence 1° is deemed equivalent to 1 day. Possibly the clue is taken from the fact that earth takes a full day-night to go round the sun.

Hence the Satya (Krita) Yuga = 4800 x 360 = 1,728,00 mortal years.

The Treta Yuga = 3600 x 360 = 1,296,00 mortal years.

The Dwapar Yuga = 2400 x 360 = 864,000 mortal years.

The Kali Yuga = 1200 x 360 = 4,32,000 mortal years.

So, one Mahayug, or great Age, including the four Yugas, being 12,000 divine years = 4,320,000 mortal years.

A thousand such Mahayugas (as mentioned) constitutes a day of Brahma and his nights are of equal durations. So a Kalpa or One Day of Brahma is equal to 4,320,000,000 mortal or human years. With in each Kalpa, 14 Manus reign; a Manvantar, or the reign of a Manu, therefore, is consequently one-fourteenth part of a Kalpa or a Day of Brahma.

In this present Kalpa, six, Manus, of whom Swayambhoo was the first, have passed away. The present being Vaivasvat. In each Manvantar, seven Rishis, certain deities on Indra and a Manu, and the Kings, their sons are created and perish. A thousand cycle of the four Yugas occur coincidentally with these Manvantars, and consequently, about 71 cycles of four Yugas elapse during each Manvantar, and measures the lives of the Manu and deities of period. At the close of this day of Brahma, a collapse of the universe takes place, which lasts through a night of Brahma, equal in duration to his day, during which period the worlds are converted into one great ocean (Pralaya)? Then the lotus born Brahma sleeps. At the end of that night he awakes and creates the creation anew.

A year of Brahma is composed of the 100 such days and nights, and a hundred of such years constitute his whole life. The period of his life is called PARA and half of it is PARADDHA or the half of a PARA. One PARADDHA or half of Brahma's duration of existence has now expired, terminating with the great Kalpa called the PADMA Kalpa. Now existing Kalpa, or a day of Brahma called Vavah Kalpa (or that of a boar) is the first of the second PARARDDHA of Brahma's existence. The dissolution which occurs at the end of each Kalpa or day of Brahma is called NAIMITTIKA, that is, incidental, occasional or contingent.

The dissolution of existing being is of three kinds: 'incidents, elemental and absolute. The first is NAIMITTIKA, occasional, incidental or Brahmya, as occasioned by the intervals of Brahma's days; the destruction of creatures, though not of the substance of the world, occurring during the night. The second is the general resolution of element into their primitive source i.e. the element of heat going back to heat that of water to water etc.) of Prakriti and occurs at the end of Brahma's life. The third, the absolute or final, Abjantika, is individual ammbilation or Moksha — that is exemption forever from future existence.

Dwelling further on time unit to determine Brahma's age the sage said: Fifteen nimeshs constitute one Kashtha, thirty Kashtha one Kala, thirty Kala one Muhurta, Three Muhurta one human day-night, thirty day-night or two such fort-nights constitute one month, six months one Ayana (northern and southern tilts of the earth round its axis) and two Ayanas make one year.

Brahma is merely part of the Vishnu or Narayan. 'Nara' means water and 'a 'Ayana' means resting place. When the earlier creation was destroyed, the world was full of water and Vishnu slept on water. That is the reason why he is called Narayan. Narayan saw that there was water all around and desired to create the new world. He, therefore, adopted the form of a boar (Varaha) and went all the way down to the wetter world. There the earth greeted him with reverence and requested him to rescue her from the neither world. Vishnu, upon being so requested, began to rear. He used his tusks to lift up the earth from the nether world. Then he carefully placed the earth on the waters. The earth floated on the oceans like a huge boat. Vishnu levelled out the earth and placed the mountains in their proper places. The earth was divided into seven regions or dweepas (continents).

"When the earth was established creation of the beings commenced. There were four types of beings that Brahma created through his psychic powers. In confusion first lot created by him was that of 'Asuras' or the demons. They came out of Brahma's thighs. Next came the gods who emerged from his mouth from Brahma's sides were created the class of Pitnis (the form the ancestors acquire after their physical dissolution.) And the human came out the last. Then he created rest of the beings."

"After that Brahma was hungry and sullen both out of the heavy toil. The demons of hunger took form and wanted to devour Brahma himself-their creator. There were some among them who did not want to eat their creator but wanted to protect him. Those who tried to protect him acquired the epithet Rakshas (from the Sanskrit term Raksha meaning to protect). And those who wanted to gobble him up came to be known as Yaksha (from the Sanskrit term yak — to eat). When Brahma saw these undesirable creatures, the hairs on his head fell off and grow up and stood up again. From these hairs were born the snakes. They acquired the name 'Ahi' because they replanted themselves after their fall. Then were created cantan perous, short-tempered yellowish beings called the Pishaach. Those who emerged from Brahma's body signify with clean voice came to be known as Gandhravas. This was followed by the emergence of the various Vedas and mantras from Brahma's four mouths."

Getting supremely enlightened by the high sage Parashara's this discourse on the creation and formations if the whole universe, Sage Maitriyas wanted to learn about the creation of the rest of the being and about the classifications of the human society. Whereupon Sage Parashar said: from Brahma's ears were created birds; from his chest sheep and from his mouth goats. From his stomach and sides there came out cattle and from his feet horses, elephants, deers and camels. Plants spouted from the bristles on Brahma's body.

"There were four classes of humans that were created: the Brahmans, the Kshatriyas, the Vaishya and the Shoodra. The Brahmans emerged from Brahma's mouth, the Kshatriyas from his arms, the Vaishyas from his thighs and the Shoodras from his feet. He also indicated ultimate destination for each category. While the Brahmans have their final destination the realm of the pitris if they behave nobly; the Kshatriya the realm of Indra (Indra-lok), the Vaishya the realm of the wind-god (Vayu-lok) and the Shoodras the realm of Gandharvas. The human life was divided into four parts: Brahmacharya (the life of learning and continence), Garhasthya (family life), Vanaprastha (preparatory period to quit society and go to jungles to dwell with nature) and Sanyas (the stage when the being feels evenly placed from all animate or inanimate beings). An ideal Brahmachari becomes a Seer, an ideal family-man attains the ancestral glory, an ideal Vanaprasthi attains to the realm of the seven Rishis and an ideal Sannyasi gets merged with the Supreme Being (Brahma) from where there is no return as that is the state of find release of the soul. Those who divide these noble persons get conquered to various hells called Tamisva, Adhatamisra, Maharauvave, Ravan Asipatravana, Ghor, Kaalsootra and Aveechika." Then the sage described the characteristics of the each yuga. The Krista or Satyayug is characterised by truth and righteousness. It is a golden age without any kind of envy and malice, deceit, sorrow, arrogance hatred, cruelty as also various other vices. In this age all the people are equal and they all worship one deity. There is only a single Veda, as creed referred to as the Brahma Yuga. The colour of Satya-Yuga is white. Men in this Yuga live for 4000 years and are physical and mental giants. There are no children to be born out of copulation and like everything else they come by mere wishing.

Treta is the age when the righteousness of the Satyayug decreases by one fourth. The colour of this yuga is red and its chief value is knowledge. The need for sacrifices and rituals begins, and men also begin to seek reward for their work. There are four Vedas instead of the one of the Satya Yuga. Man live for 3000 years; procreation is carried out by mere touching.

Dwapar is the age when righteousness exists in only half of the amount as it existed in the Satyayuga. The colour of the Yuga is yellow, and the main virtue is sacrifice. Only a few adhere to duty or truth for its own sake. Diseases, misery and calamity begin and the castes also come into existence. The scriptures of this age are the Puranas. Men in it live for 2000 years and progeny can come only after copulation which should be pure and legal. In this age a man can have only one lawful wife; there is only one time at which marriage can take place; the time when the girls or would be wives start mestruating.

Kaliyug[3] refers to the present age of mankind. In this age righteousness is now only one fourth of what it was in Satyayuga. True

---

[3] According to other scriptured sources the Kaliyug is believed to have begun at midnight between 17 and 18th February 3102 BC i.e., at the time when the Pandava Arjuna's grandson Pariskshit ascended to the throne of Hastinapur. This being says that we are living in the 6th millennium of the Kaliyug and there are still 427,000 years to go before this age ends, at which point Lord Vishnu will appear in the Kalki Incarnation to destroy the world through flood and fire.

worship cease to exist in this age. The Tantra-Shashtra or those branches of knowledge whose ultimate aim is to satiate all physical desires become main scriptures. The colour of this age is said to be black. Men live to variable ages and a few crores 100 years. It is the age of anger, hatred, lust, creed, passion, pride, strife and discard. There is universal viciousness and weakness with all kinds of diseases afflicting people. Youth no longer respect their elders and there is excessive pre-occupation with things material or physical. Men seek satisfaction outside the bonds of marriage. Women of loose morals far exceed the virtuous.

Each Yuga is supposed to be preceded by a period called its Sandhya (transitional phase or moving twilight) and is followed by a period called Sandhyamha (evening twilight).

Pralaya (The End)

The sage said: "At the end of a thousand periods (cycles) of the four ages the earth is for the most part exhausted. A total death then ensues which last a hundred years, and in consequence of the failure of getting food all things become languid and exanimate, and at last entirely perish. The eternal Vishnu then assumes the character of Rudra, the destroyer and descends to reunite all his creatures with himself. He enters into the seven rays of the sun drinks up all the waters of the globe, and causes all moisture whatever in living bodies or in the soil, to evaporate, thus drying up the whole earth. The seas and the rivers, the mountain torrents and springs are all exhaled, and so are the waters of Patal (hither world).

Thus fed, through his instruction, with abundant moistures, the seven solar rays dilate to twelve suns, whose radiance goes above, below, and on every side, and sits the three worlds (the earth, the heaven and the patal lok) on fire. The three worlds, consumed by these suns, become rugged and deformed throughout the whole extent of their mountains, rivers and seas; and the earth, bare of greenery and destitute of moisture, done remains, resembling in appearance the back of a tortoise. The destroyer of all things, Hari, in the form of Rudra, like the all destroying flames of fire, becomes the scorbing breath of the serpent Sesha, and thereby first reduces the Patal to ashes.

The great fire, when it has burnt all the divisions of Patal proceeds to earth and consumes it also. A vast whirlpool of adding flames then spreads to the regions of the atmosphere and the sphere of the gods, and wraps them in ruin. The three spheres show like a frying pan amidst the surrounding flames, that prey upon all moveable or stationary things. The inhabitants of the two upper spheres, having discharged their functions, and being annoyed by the heat, remove to the spheres above or Maharloka. When that becomes heated, its inhabitants, who after the full period of their stay, are desirous of ascending to higher regions, depart for Janloka (the realm of the devotees). Those saintly mortals who have delightly worshipped Vishnu and are distinguished for piety, abide at the time of dissolution in Maharloka with the Pitras (proglinators), the Manu and the seven Rishis, the various orders of celestial spirits and the gods. These, when the heat of the flames that destroy the world reach to Maharloka, repair to Janaloka in their subtle form, destined to become re-embodied in similar capacity in their former form, when the world is renewed, at the beginning of the succeeding Kalpa. This continues throughout the life of Brahma. At the expiration of his life all are destroyed but those who have attained a residence in the Brahamloka, by having identified themselves in spirit with the Supreme, are finally revolved into the role existing Brahma. Janardana (Vishnu) in the form of Rudra, having consumed the whole world breaths forth heavy clouds. Mighty in size and loud in thunder, they fell all space. Showing down torrents of water, then clouds quench the dreadful fires which involve the three worlds and then they rain without interruption for a hundred years and deluge the whole universe. Pouring down in drops as large as a big hall, these rains overspread the earth, and fill the middle regions and inundates heaven. The world is now enveloped in darkness, and all things animate or inanimate, having perished, the clouds continue to pour down waters for more than a hundred years.

"Then again peace returns, waters begin to subside, the Supreme spirit in the form of Vishnu reigns from whose navel the primal lotus having Brahma seated in it. And then Brahma restarts the process of creation by planting the life-germ in the 'matter' of the earth, and sets in motion the evolution of life through — like the ancient times-from the fish living in the water, to tortoise. Then, the process of incarnations of Vishnu restarts whenever the order of nature is threatened by the rise of the evil forces and decay of the noble volumes."

The Lakshmi Episode

Having created the world, Brahma also wanted to create a son who would be just like him. As he thought about it, a son appeared on his lap. Since the child kept on crying Brahma called it Rudra [in Sanskrit 'nud' is the roof from which is formed rudan' which means to cry or weep]. The child, however, began to cry again and did not stop till Brahma gave it seven names which are Mahesha, Bhava, Sarva, Pashupati, Bhima, Ugra and Mahadeva besides the original name Rudra. This child eventually came to be known as Lord Shankar. He was married to Sati, the daughter of Daksha Prajapati. But owing to her father showing disrespect to her husband, she consigned her body in the second pit of the sacrifice held by Daksha to celebrate his acquiring the status of being the progenitor. Subsequently Lord Shiv married Uma, the daughter of Himvant (the ruler of the Himalayas).

Mahadeva's one psychic Progeny was sage Durvasa the sage renowned for his foul temper. Once upon a time, Durvasa was wandering around the world and he happened to spot a very fragrant garland of flowers in the hands of a pretty woman. Durvasa wanted to have that garland which the woman gladly did. Placing that sweet-fragrance emanating garland upon his head, Durvasa happened to roam about the world. As he was roaming about he spotted Indra astride on his famous mount Eiravat, and accompanied by other gods, coming to his side. Durvasa picked up the garland and threw it at Indra. Indra placed it on the head on his mount Eiravat. The mighty elephant was bewildered receiving such a powerful and enchanting fragrance coming from something on its head. When he raised his trunk to get a better snuff, the movement of its head caused the garland slip down its head to fall on the ground where it was casually tramphed over by the king Pachyder.

Durvasa who was still not far away blew up in rage. How could this mere chief of the gods dare dishonour the garland that he chose to gift him? He thought as if Indra had deliberately insulted him. Instead of showing gratitude for receiving such rare and soft-fragrance emanating garland, the divine' chief in his arrogance had the gift trampled underfoot. Durvasa then cursed him:" O Indra! You are getting arrogant in the power and prosperity you wield. Now I curse you that Lakshmi, the goddess of prosperity, so far thriving in your heaven shall desert it for ever. And you shall instant by become powerless. Although realising his mistake Indra had tried to apologise before Durvasa, the sage known for his fiery temperament had hunted his curse on the divine chief.

Crest fallen and repentful when Indra reached back Amaravati, his capital, he was dismayed to find it to be dreamy and dilapidated with all grace and magnificence missing. Following the sage's curse Lakshmi, the source of all prosperity and riches had left his realm. The plants were drying and the flowers were withering on their stalks. No where sacrifices were performed and the whole realm appeared dying. So was the state of the earth and all the realms which were under the gods rule. The gods quickly assembled to find a solution to the given problem they were facing. They knew that if their arch enemies learnt about their losing all power and key they would be attacking them in as time. Now they apprehended that their crushing defeat was round the corner. What should they do? Immediately they made fire-god-Agni-their leader and repaired to Brahma for refuge and help. But Brahma expressed his in ability to render them any help.Instead, he advised them to seek help from Lord Vishnu, the ultimate saviour of the gods and the noble. The gods immediately gathered on the northern shore of the great ocean and began to pray. Vishnu was touched by their feelingful prayer and manifested himself before the gods. He advised them after hearing their tale of woe:" Lakshmi has disappeared deep into the oceans. Unless the oceans are churned. She cannot be recovered. But alone you all cannot churn the huge span of the oceans. You must seek temporary truce with the demons and make them agree to churn the ocean. If the ocean could be properly churned, out emerge from it will be Amrita drinking which you all shall become immortal." Vishnu also assured that he would see to it that Amrita was not imbibed by any of the demons though the gods must openly offer the demons an equitable share of the Amrita. Then Vishnu also advised them to procure. Mount Mander to use it as the churning stick and Serpent Vasuki to be used as the churning rope.

When the gods made the offer before the demons tempted by the Amrita they readily agreed. On the advice of Vishnu the gods and demons hurled into the ocean choices herbs before commencing its churning. The gods as advised by Vishnu grasped Vasuki's tail while the demons grasped the head of the serpent. The pressure on the serpents' body caused toxic fumes and flames to emerge from Vasuki's mouths. These distressed the demons quietly but tempted by Amrita drinking possibility they endured the ordeal. However, the gases that came out of the snake's mouth went up in sky and formed clouds. These clouds were driven towards the tail of the snake and poured down soothing rain on the gods. However, there was a persisting disturbance: the Mandar was getting frequently imbalanced due to its floating on the water. Since it needed a firm base, Vishnu assumed the form of a massive birth on which the mount was placed. This facilitated both the groups to continue churning non-stop.

And soon wonderful objects began to emerge from the ocean as a result of the churning. The first to come out was the cow Surabhi, worshipped by the gods. Then it was followed by many rare objects and beings including the most toxic poison 'halahala' which at the joint request of both demons and the gods was imbibed by Lord Shiva but he didn't allow it to go down his neck. But the fierce toxicity of the poison made his neck turn blue. Hence his acquiring yet another epithets for himself: 'Neelkantha'. Since he had imbibed the most poisonous drinks of the universe for the benefit of all animate and inanimate being he came to be universally hailed as 'Mahadeva' (Super-god). Lakshmi also emerged but she sought the hand of Lord Vishnu. The moon also emerged which

Lord Shiva accepted to place this Cool luminary on his head so that he could get relief from the heat created by toxic 'halahal'. The last to emerge was Dhanvantari, clad in dazzling white notes and holding the pot of Amrita in his hands. The gods and demons were delighted to have received the desired object. They began to fight for Amrita but Vishnu managed to make only the gods have it and not the demons.

The sages began to chant hymns seeing the goddess of prosperity recovered from the ocean depths. The Gandharvas sang and the Apsaras danced. It is mentioned that the body rivers like Ganga also reached there to welcome Lakshmi. Mythologically it is believed that there are eight king-elephants, which guard the eight directions. These elephants took clear water from golden vessels and bathed the goddess. The oceans' personified form appeared as well to present Lakshmi a garland of lotus flowers of undecayable quality. The divine architect Vishwakarma provided the jewels. These bathed dressed and garlanded Lakshmi chose Vishnu as her eternal espouse. Since the goddess of prosperity, Lakshmi, has ever kind with the gods as she was unpopular with the demon. Now her choosing Vishnu finally made the demon all the more angry. Not only that, Vishnu, by adopting the Mohini (Enchantress's) form also tactfully deprived the demons of even the Amrita and made this unique portion shared only by the gods. Having drunk the Amrita the gods again became powerful and routed demons out of their capital Amravati. Finally no other place to stay either in the Swarga or the earth, the demons descended to the another world (Patal). The gods were delighted. They bowed before Vishnu and Continued to rule over heaven. The sun resumed is normal duty of lighting the universe. The stars also followed suit. The chief of gods, Indra, ascended to his throne after praying Lakshmi devotedly by chanting the following eight verses.

Indra Uvacha:

> **Namastestu Mahamaye Shreepeethe Surpoojite**
> **Shankha Chakra gada haste Mahalakshmi namostute || 1 ||**

Indra said: O Grand Goddess, seated on the exalted pedestal and worshipped by the gods! I bow to thee! O Mahalakshmi! Weilding conch, chakra (discus) and mace in your hands! I salute you **|| 1 ||**

Namaste Garudaroodhe Kolasurbhayankari !
Sarva Pap hare Devi, Mahalakshmi namoustute || 2 ||

O Goddess Mahalakshmi! Riding on Garuda, frightening the demon called Kolasur and remover of all sin, I bow to thee || 2 ||

Sarvagye sarva-varade sarvadushtabhayankari !
Sarvadukhhare Devi Mahalakshmi namostute || 3 ||

O Goddess Mahalakshmi! You are Omniscient, you grant boons to all and frighten all the wicked! You are the remover of all sorrows; I bow to thee || 3 ||

Siddhibuddhiprade Devi bhuktimuktipradayani !
Mantrapoote sada Devi Mahalakshmi namostute || 4 ||

O Great goddess Lakshmi! Purified by the Mantra, you grant to your devotees' wisdom, capacities to attain perfection and indulge in enjoyment and you are the one who grants final emancipation to their souls or the Moksha || 4 ||

Adyaantarahite Devi Adyashaktimaheshwari !
Yogje yogasambhoote Mahalakshmi namostute || 5 ||

O Goddess, without any beginning or end, the Primal Power! O Grand Deity! Manifest only through the concentrated devotion! I bow to thee! || 5 ||

Sthoolasookshma Maharaudre Mahashakti mahodare !
Mahapaphare Devi Mahalakshmi namostute || 6 ||

O Goddess! You are visibly manifest but also subtly existent, and you have terrible appearance! You are the primal power, having great capacity to end severest afflictions. O Great Goddess! I bow to thee! || 6 ||

Padmasanashthite Devi Parbrahmaswaroopini !
Parameshi jagan matar Mahalakshmi namostute || 7 ||

Seated on the lotus flower, O manifest form of the Supreme Being! O Goddess! O Supreme Goddess! Mother of the World! O Mahalakshmi! I bow to thee! || 7 ||

Shwetambar-dhare Devi nanalankara- bhooshite !
Jagatisthite jaganmatar Mahalakshmi namostute || 8 ||

O Goddess! You are clad in the white clothes and decorated with many garments! You instinct the whole world by your presence and all the realms come into being by your grace. O Mahalakshmi! I bow to thee || 8 ||

Parashar then told Maitreya: Indra's prayers pleased and propitiated Lakshmi and she agreed to grant him boons. The first boon that Indra asked for was that Lakshmi should never leave the three worlds. And the Second boon was that Lakshmi should never turn away anyone who prayed to Lakshmi using the same prayer that Indra had worshipped the goddess with. Hence Lakshmi's also incarnating herself whenever Vishnu incarnate Himself to remove the distress of the noble and subdue the evil forces.

The Story of Dhruva

Maitreya asked: "O great Sage (Parashar). Now tell me about the creation night from Bhrigu's, progeny to the present date."

Parashar replied: "You know that Sage Bhrigu was married to Khyati and their union brought forth the existence of two male issues Dhata and Vidhata and a daughter called Lakshmi. Dhata and Vidhata were respectively married to Mahatma Manu's two daughters: Aayati and Niyati who begot two sons Prana and Mrikundu who were the agents of Dyutiman and Markandeya. Dyutiman produced Rajvan and Markandey Vedshira. This is how the creation continued to develops.

From Brahma's body was created Manu. Manu is the source of all human creation. Hence the terms Manav or Manuj for man which literally mean the products of Manu. Manu had two righteous and brave sons known as Priyavarta and Uttanapad. Uttanapad had two wives Suruchi and Suniti. Suruchi's son was Uttama and Suniti's Dhruva. Since Suruchi was more beautiful, Uttanapad was more fond of her. Hence his affection on Suruchi's son, Uttama, was more than what he showered on Dhruva, the son of Suniti.

One day, while moving in the royal court, Dhruva found Uttama sitting on the father's lap on the throne. He also longed to sit there. While he was trying Suruchi, who was standing close by, scolded him sharply saying that he shouldn't covet for the throne since Uttama was its eventual occupant. She also reprimanded Dhruva for trying to get something which was not his.

Dhruva was feeling hurt so he went straight to his mother Suniti and narrated her the whole incident. Hearing it Suniti tried to console her son: "Dear son! One gets in this life in accordance with what one had done in the previous lives. Suruchi and Uttama must have done better deeds in previous lives than what we did to deserve the position they enjoy. Instead of craving for Uttama's position you should try to do better deeds so that in the coming life you may continue to get honourable position. If you do good deeds, act righteously and religiously there is no reason why you shouldn't get better position than that what Uttama enjoys in the life."

Dhruva fell quite consoled with his mother's words. He said:" Mother! Your words have given me peace. I will try to achieve the highest position of all. True, the king loves Uttam's mother more and it is also true that I am not her son. But I am your son and I will show you what I can achieve. I don't crave for the throne. Let Uttama have it. I will achieve a place by my hard work and devotion which may even be unachievable been for high sages and seers."

The determination in the boy's words was apparent. Although Suniti tried to dissuade him from going to the forest to perform a severe penance, Dhruva would not listen to her. The forest was not far away from the palace. When Dhruva reached the denser part of the jungle he met seven sages. He bowed before them and said: "I am Dhruva, the son of Raja Uttanapad and Suniti. I am unhappy and so I have come before you." The sages were surprised and they asked: "Prince, you are hardly five years old. What could be the reason of your feeling so unhappy at this age. Moreover, your father is a king and very much on throne. Nor you seem to be suffering from any illness. Then what could have caused as much unhappiness to you as to drive you out of the luxury of the palace and to these jungles?"

Then Dhruva elaborately told them the reason of unhappiness. He said that he desired neither wealth nor kingdom. He simply wanted to achieve a position no one has achieved before. Seeing his determination writ large on his face, the sages were amazed. Such a quietly resolve in such a juvenile mind! But they knew the firmness of a child's resistance or 'Baal Hath! They know that if a child decides to achieve anything nothing can prevent it. So, instead of discouraging him or dissuading him from performing rigorous penance in the dense jungle, they advised him to worship Vishnu for only Vishnu could assure Dhruva the position that he desired. While departing they taught him the 12-syllabled mantra: 'OM NAMO BHAGAVATE VASUDEVAYA' which they told was very efficient to please Vishnu.

As they departed, Dhruva continued his journey onwards to reach the Madhuvan on the banks of river Yamuna. Many years later this region was to be known as Mathura to be established by Rama's younger brother, Shatrughna after killing Madhu demon's son Lavana. Selecting a neat spot right on the bank of Yamuna under a huge tree; he started his worship of Lord Vishnu, chanting the Mantra continuously. However, not many days elapsed when Dhruva's severe penance began to cause a stir in the divine realm. As has always been the case, Indra got nervous seeing Dhruva's this penance whose ultimate aim he thought was to capture his (Indra's) throne. Immediately many kinds of obstruction were devised by the celestials at Indras behest. Apsaras (divine danseuses) were dispatched followed by deadly 'rakshashas! The divine inspiration made Jackals start howling around Dhruva. Ghost and gobbins came to frighten the boy. But Dhruva remained undisturbed. Concentrating only on Lord Vishnu he continued to chant the Mantra: OM NAMO BHAGVATE VASUDEVAYA!

When the gods' activities failed to disturb Dhruva's concentration they grew panicky. They were now convinced that Dhruva must be eyeing at some divine status either of sun, Kubera, Varuna and others. At last they went to Vishnu and requested him to devise some plan as to make Dhruva stop his worship. Without bandying words with the gods, Vishnu reassured the gods that they shouldn't feel disturbed. He knew that such positions and material rewards were the last things in Dhruva's mind. In fact Vishnu had allowed the gods to devise all obstructions to Dhruva's worship with two intentions. First, to ascertain the firmness in Dhruva worship and secondly, to make the gods realise that there were other positions much respectable then their own position. Having served his both the purposes he decided to appear before Dhruva. So one fine morning Vishnu appeared before Dhruva and offered him a boon. The boy opened his eyes and saw Vishnu standing before him. Dhruva sought the boon that he should always feel like praying to Vishnu. As a matter of fact, Dhruva didn't really wanted a boon at all. When he saw Lord Vishnu before him, he desired nothing more. All his yearning seemed totally gratified. Nevertheless, Vishnu was so pleased with Dhruva's devotion and selfless dedication that he persisted in granting Dhruva some boon. When persistently asked to reveal his desire this way Dhruva, at last, said that he wanted a position as might place him on the top of the world.

Vishnu assured Dhruva of his getting such a position. He also told Dhruva that in an earlier life Dhruva had been a Brahman who was devoted to Vishnu. Since Brahman friend was a wealthy prince he desired to get the same position and so Dhruva was born in this life as a prince.

However, in this life Dhruva desired no such mundane status or wealth, Lord Vishnu promised to make him occupy such an eternal position in the sky as would make all the stars revolve round it. His mother Suniti, by the virtue of her being Dhruva's mother, got also a high position in the heaven not far from Dhruva's son.

[The place of the Dhruva Tara or the Pole. Star can still be easily identified. Near the Ursa Major (Saptarishi Mandal) is placed the Pole Star which is the Star of Dhruva. This Pole-Star remains stationary for a very long period of time.]

The Story of The Kings Vena and Prithu

Dhruva subsequently married and he produced two sons of the wedlock named Shishti and Bhavya. While Bhavya in due time produced one son Shambhu but Shishti from his wife Suchhaya got five sons: Ripu, Rupunjaya, Vipra, Vrikala and Vrikateja. Ripu got married to Vrihati and they got a son called Chakshusa, who married to Prajapati's daughter Pushkarini. This pair produced Manu who got married to Vairaj's daughter Nadavala and produced ten brilliant sons: Kuru, Puru, Shata-dymna, Tapasvi, Satyavan, Shuchi, Agnitom, Atiratri, Sudymna and Abhimanyu. The eldest son Kuru married to Aagneyee and this pair produced six sons. Anga, Sumana, Khyati, Kratu, Angira and Shivi. Among these it was Angira who married to Suneetha and they produced Vena. Vena had produced Prithu who had exploited all the natural resources of the earth to the hilt for the people's welfare. In fact Prithu was produced from Vena's right hand when it was kneeded vigorously by the sages.

Hearing about Vena's hand's kneeding to produce Prithu, Maitreya developed a natural curiosity. He asked: "What were those special circumstances which made the sages kneed Vena's hand to produce Prithu to continue this lineage?" Upon this Parashar said: "Dear! The truth is that Anga's wife Suneetha was the daughter of death-god. Hence Suneetha also developed some vicious qualities of her parents, which were also inherited by her son, Vena.

In fact Vena was not a good king at all as he ascended to the throne he declared that no deities should be worshipped, nor any sacrifices should be held to propitiate them. He also prevented the worship of Lord Vishnu since he claimed himself to be superior to that Supreme Lord. Although the sages tried to persuade the king to change his way but Vena just didn't care for their advice since he was arrogant and tyrant by nature.

At last the sages decided that this arrogant king should die as he was threatening the very system and order of the creation. With this resolve in their mind they took a straw charged it with their holy incantation and hurled it aiming at vena. He died in a trice. But, having killed him the sages realised that there was none to rule the state. Vena didn't have any progeny so the throne was unoccupied. With no king available anarchy was the natural consequence. But devising a Mantra again they decided to produce a child out of the dead king's body. The sages then began to knee the dead king's thighs. After much kneeding and chanting of the holy mantra there emerged a dwarf like existence from his thighs.

"What shall I do?" asked the Dwarf.

"Sit", said the sages and with this term, 'Nishad', which means to no in Sanskrit[1], the dwarf.

Came to be known as Nishada. Later on, the sons of Nisheda came to dwell in the Vindhya Mountains.

When Nishada departed the sages thought that their purpose was not served. So then again began to kneed the dead-body's right hand. And then emerged a shining man from the second kneeding. This was named Prithu. As he was born, a divine bow, arrows and armour fell on him from the spies. Everyone was happy at Prithu's birth. Since he was Vena's progeny, the dead king's soul was not to be consigned to hell. Because going by the accepted norm an issueless person's soul has to carry this stigma since it doesn't get oblation from its progeny. Nevertheless place downed everywhere at Prithu's birth and his getting the divine approval in the form of the bow and the arrows. The rivers and the oceans also arrived to fill water at the due places. They also

---

[1] Hence the term 'Upa-nished' literally means sit closely

brought jewels and garlands for Prithu's coronation. Soon after there arrived all the gods led by Brahma. Brahma noticed that Prithu had the mark of CHAKRA (Lord Vishnu's Weapon) on his right hand. This was an auspicious sign because it meant that Prithu was descended from Vishnu. This is believed to be truly a divine sign, as even the gods cannot rival with those that carry this sign on their body.

Following these events, Prithu was ritually crowned. He proved to be a powerful king. The waters of the ocean trembled when he passed and even the most sturdy mountains allowed a passage for him out of his sheer awe. He proved to be so mighty a ruler that his flag ever flew unbowered. By his authority even the earth yielded crops without any ploughing. The cows gave a lot of milk and the flowers were full of honey. As soon as he was appointed the king he arranged for a sacrifice. It was from this sacrificial endeavour that 'Sutas' and the Meghadas (a kinds of race of the birds) were born who constantly chanted songs in the praise of their king.

However, as the sages tried very hard yet there was a short gap between Vena's death and Prithu's birth. In that interval the earth was ruler-less. And it is a well-known fact that the land does not flourish in the absence of a king. Consequently, due to that short absence of the king on the earth the herbs and other priceless vegetation disappeared from the earth. Since in those time the people of the earth mostly survived on them, they were hungry. Then these people went to Prithu and begged him to restore the herbs. To revive them on the earth, Prithu took up his bow and arrows and began to chase the earth who ran away from him in the form of a cow. But wherever it went Prithu Chased it with the bow and arrows in his hand. Eventually Prithu caught up with the earth and the earth restored to whatever few herbs were left. In order to ensure that the earth returned to normalcy and again became fertile, Prithu levelled out the mountains with his mighty bow. Earlier to him the creation had no human settlements, cities, village etc. or grains or anything. It was Prithu who made the earth dwellable. Hence one of the epithets earth is known by is Prithvi which literally means of Prithu.'

The Birth of The Prachitas

Prithu's sons were Antardhan and Veda. Antardhan got married to Shikhandian and they produced a son-called Havirdhan. He married to the girl of the fire dynasty called Dheeshana and their union produces six sons: Prachinvarbi Shukra, Gaya, Krishna, and Vrija and Ajin. The eldest Prachinvarbi married the daughter of the ocean Savarna.

Out of this wedlock were produced the sons called the Prachetas. They accomplished very different penance (Tapasya) for the thousand years under the ocean.

At this point Maitreya again asked Parashara : "Why did the Prachetas perform difficult penance for the thousand years?" Parashar's answer was the following.

Brahma had advised Prachinvarbi to ensure that the world become full of people. Prachinvarbi in turn, passed on this advise to his sons. But the Prachetas didn't know how to go about this task. Then their father advised them to pray to Lord Vishnu since the Lord was only competent to solve all problems. It was after praying to Vishnu that Brahma had created the universe at the beginning of the original creation. Getting these instructions from their father the Prachetas prayed for or did penance for the thousand years.

It was when the stipulated period of the penance was over, Lord Vishnu appeared before them astride his mount the bird Garud. On being offered the boon by the Lord the Prachetas requested that they should be made capable to people the world. After obtaining the desired boon when the Prachetas emerged from the ocean they found that, in their absence, the earth had been totally covered by the trees. So thick had been their growth that no winds could blow. Getting emerged at the audacity of the trees the Prachetas Created wind and fire from their mouths. The winds uprooted the trees and the fire burnt them. With the result, the trees began to be destroyed speedily.

Now, sun or the moon, the king of all the vegetation on the earth, couldn't bear this outrage to its subjects. At once he rushed to the Prachetas and tried to appease them. The moon even offered Manisha — a girl who had been born from the trees and whom, Soma had boutingly brought up in marriage to the Prachetas. The moon also promised them that their son from Manisha would be Daksha who would be the progemeter of all the people in the world. Getting the promise to have a son for people in the world they were appeared. But they wanted to know more about this mysterious girl Manisha. Then Soma told the Pracheta the story of Manisha's birth.

Long long times ago, there was a sage called Kandu. Once this sage was performing a very difficult penance on the bank of the river Gomati. Getting apprehensive of the sage's objective of the Tapasya-lest it be the divine throne. Indra sent an apsara (a divine danseuse) named Pramlocha to disturb the sage's concentration. Being a very charming and beautiful woman, Kandu fell in love with her almost instantly and married her. They then lived together for more than a hundred years in a valley in the mountain, Mandara, enjoying their honeymoon. When more then a century passed the apsara desired to return to her abode in the heaven. But Kandu insisted "Stay for some more time". She agreed and stayed again for about a hundred years. After this she again expressed her desire to return to heaven. But Kandu, unable to hear separation from him, said "Stay for some more time".

And this way they passed uncountable years in their lovely sojourn. After a long period Kandu regained his senses. He said to Pramlocha. "Dear! one whole day is over. It is now evening. Let me do my Sandhya (or say evening prayers)"

'One day', she exclaimed in amazement. "Aren't you aware that we have passed many centuries together. To be precise nine hundred and eighty seven years six months and three days have passed since you married me." Kandu was bewildered. He didn't know that such a long period had elapsed to his marriage with Pramlocha. He immediately went back to his Tapasya and allowed Pramlocha to return to heaven. On her way towards heaven, Pramlocha wiped her sweat on the leaves of the tree. Since she was bearing a baby it also came out with the sweat and was left with the trees. It was this baby that eventually became Manisha in due time.

Why was she married to ten persons (ten Prachetas) also had an interesting explanation. In an earlier life Manisha had been married to a king. But the king died early leaving Manisha a youthful and charming widow. The young widow had prayed to Vishnu through a long penance and Vishnu was propitiated by her worship. Then the widow had desired the boon that she might have a son like Brahma and that she might have good many husbands in several lives. Vishnu gave his word that she would have a son like Brahma and that she would have several good husbands in the same life. Hence Manisha's, marriage to the ten Prachetas.

As promised by Soma (the moon) Daksha was eventually born. He was the same Daksha who in his earlier life was the son of Brahma. In due time Daksha grew young and then following his marriage he got sixty daughters. Ten of them were married to Dharma (Dharamaraj or the death-god, the master of all souls), thirteen to the primeval sage. Kashyap, twenty-seven to Chandra (the moon) four to Arishtaname, two to Angiras (the divine sage) and two to Krishasha. The thirteen daughters who were married to Kashyap were Aditi, Diti, Danu, Kala, Arishtha, Surasa, Surabhi, Vanita, Tamra, Krodhavasha, Ira, Kadnu and Muni.

[In fact these daughter are believed to be the mothers of the various species that came to dwell on the earth. While Aditi was the mother of the gods (also called Aditya which literally means 'of Aditi') the demons' (also called Daitya or of Diti) mother was Diti; those of snakes and reptiles Kadnu and those of birds Vanita]

Kashyapa was the sine of all creation. His union with Diti had produced two brave sons called Hiranyakashyapa and Hiranyaksha. Hiranyakashyapa was the progenitor of the demon race. His sons were Anublada, Hlada, Prahlad and Sanblada. Among these Prahlad earned a special renown for being a demon lord yet a staunch devotee of Lord Vishnu.

The Story of Prahlad

Hiranykashyapa was a powerful demon and a determined person. He performed very severe penance to please Brahma. His determination made Brahma appear before him, fully propitiated, and the creator asked the demon to have his boon. He demanded that he should not be slayed either by man or god or beast, neither in the day or in the night; neither out-side the home or inside it and neither on the land or in water. He eventually had this boon which made him almost invincible. He conquered the three worlds; driving out Indra from heaven he assured himself the lordship of even the divinities. He also assumed the titles of Savita, Vayu, Agni, Varuna, Kubera, Yama and the rest of the gods. He routed the gods out of heaven when roamed about here and there shelterless. Hiranyakshyapa was now the sole authority in the Universe. Everyone had to worship him. He was now the master of all progeny of Kashyap sage. Now he lived in a magnificent palace made of crystals. He enjoyed all the pleasures of three worlds, to the hilt.

He had four sons but his third, son Prahlad was a precocious child. He learnt his lessons fast and while going through the ancient accounts he developed intense devotion for Vishnu. When he returned home from his guru's place where he was staying to gain knowledge, Hiranyakashyapa asked: "What did you learn there?"

'I have learnt to pray Vishnu', the boy Prahlad replied rather proudly.

Hirankyakashpa was enraged. How could that silly teacher teach him to pray my arch enemy" he thought. Immediately he summoned the teacher and questioned him.

'No, I have not told anything about Vishnu', the teacher defended himself. 'He must have learnt about our race's enemy of his own accord'.

Then the demon lord asked his son again: "Dear son, who has taught you this rubbish?"

'The teacher of all teachers, Lord Vishnu himself, was the reply.

'Who is Vishnu?'

'Lord of my heart and the master of this entire universe.'

'Lord and Master... my foot? How can there be any one else when I am here?' The demon lord blurted out rather pompously.

'He is your lord as well !' replied the defiant boy.

Hiranyakashyapa blew up. "Take him away", thundered the king. "Tell the teacher to weed out all this misleading knowledge from his mind?

Although Prahlad was sent back and taught the lessons afresh with greater emphasis on the Sage Shukracharya's, policies which normally guided the demon race, the devotion of Vishnu couldn't be taken away from his psyche. So when he came to the palace and Hiranyakashyapa again asked as to what he had studied, Prahlad's reply was: "To pray to Vishnu."

Hearing this reply. The demon-lord thundered: "Kill this evil boy. No good will come to the race of demons by his staying alive. He is a disgrace to my family."

Getting this royal order a variety of the tricks were employed to kill that boy Prahlad. He was thrown before the 'must' elephants, extremely poisonous snakes were let loose on him; all kinds of weapons were targetted at him but by the grace of Lord Vishnu Prahlad emerged from every vile trick unscathed. In fact neither the snakes could bite him nor the weapons could touch his body. Then he was thrown from the high hills into the ocean, but he emerged from the waters chanting the Mantra: "OM NAMO BHAGVATE VASUDEVAYA" more radiant and healthy than ever before. Even the attempt to poison his food couldn't kill him because reaching inside his body resounding with Vishnu's name even the toxic material became ambrosial. In fact the more the demon tried to kill him the healthier he emerged after every ordeal.

Hiranyakashyapa was getting mad in anger. Though said to be the most powerful existence in the three worlds he was unable to kill his own adolescent son. At last his sister, Holika, came to his help. She said, "Dear Brother! I have received a boon on the strength of which I am immense to any effect of fire. Now I will sit on a burning pyre with Prahlad in my lap so that he may be incinerated to ashes. And I would not get burnt because of the virtue of that boon.

So, accordingly the pyre was arranged. Holika sat on it with her nephew Prahlad in her lap and the pyre was sat on fire. And to and behold, despite that boon Holika was incinerated while Prahlad emerged unscathed, chanting the name of Vishnu. Again Hiranyakashyapa tried to have his son brainwashed. He sent to him to the teacher with the clear instructions to effect any memory from his mind of Lord Vishnu. Though the demon priests tried their level best, Prahlad returned to the palace without any change in his demeanour.

Hiranyakashyapu again asked Prahlad: "My son! Tell me what policy one should adopt to deal with friends. And how to tackle one's foes?"

Prahlad: "Father! I deem that there it no foe in the world. The whole universe is instinct with one Existence. Lord Vishnu is in everything. He is in the demons and the deities, the good and bad, the animate and inanimate. Since he is in every one how can you classify anyone as our foe? My Lord Supreme permeates every list of this creation!"

Now the Demon-Lord lose his cool. He got up from his throne. Thundering he ordered: "Tie this boy with a rope around this pillar. Now I will behead him with my sword.

Prahlad was still insisted: "Father, my Lord Vishnu is also in this pillar as well as in your sword." But soon the boy was tied as instructed by Hiranyakashyapa. As the King came close to behead Prahlad with his sword, suddenly the column of stone had burst asunder and out emerged from it a bizarre existences having man-like body and lion like face. That was Narsimha Avatar of Lord Vishnu. Immediately that man-lion held Hiranyakashyapu by the gruff and took him to the threshold of the building. It was neither the day-time nor night, it was twilight. Taking the king to the threshold the man-lion sat on a stone and placed the king on his lap — This ensured that neither the king's body was on the land or in water. Then the man-lion incarnation of Vishnu tore apart Hiranayakashyapa from the middle. He had killed the demon-Lord circumventing every condition that the Hiranayakashyapa had put forth while asking the boon of immortality from Brahma. He was killed at twilight, by a man-lion almost in the middle of air.

Meanwhile Prahlad kept on chanting Vishnu's name. The Narshimha left after giving boon to Prahlad and staying Hiranyakshyapa. After Hiranyakashyapa's death Prahlad became the king of the Daityas. He ruled well and very wisely. For the first time there was an amicable peace between the demons and the deities. Subsequently Prahlad married and produced many sons and grandson. One of Prahald's son was Virochana and Virochana's son was Vali, a king renowned for his charity. Vali had a powerful son-called Vanasur who was a peerless warrior.

Details of other Species

Sage Kashyapa's another wife, name was Danu who came to be known as mother of all Danavas [yet another variety of demons]. Prominent among the Danavas was Shambar, Ayonmikh, Shankushira, Ekachakra, Mohabahu, Tarak, Mahabal, Vinishakarva, Pulram and Viprachitti. The most famous among them was Vinishakarva who had three daughters named Sharmishta, Upadans and Hayashira. Viprachitra married to Sinbika whose most prominent son was a danava who has backed into two pieces by Vishnu's Chakra at the time of the Churning of The ocean and both parts became the danava: Rahu and Ketu. Kashya sage's yet another wife was Tamara who begot six daughters. Which are believed to be the mother of a variety of birds like parrot and crows, falcons, and of the quadrapeds like horses, camels' etc. This way all the species of the world — said to be 840 million owe their origin to Kashyapa sage. This spell of creation existed during Swanochish Manvantar whose details will be given ahead.

The Story of Priyavarta and Bharat and Details about Hells and Heavens

Getting the details sage Maitreya asked sage Parashar: "Sir! You have told about Manu Priyavarta and Uttanapad. While you have disclosed me history about Uttanapad's son-Dhruva, you have not told me anything about Priyavarta's progeny. Kindly enlighten me about that too."

Parashar then told him about Priyavarta's dynasty. Priyavarta married the daughter of Kandarma and had ten sons. Their names were Agnidhra, Agnivahu, Vakushamana, Dyutimana, Putra, Medha Medhatithi, Bhavya, Savana, Putra and Jyotishmana. Jyotishmana were not interested in becoming kings, so they became sages.

Then the whole earth was divided into seven charnas called Dveepa. Priyavarta gave each of the remaining seven sons a dveepa to rule over. Agnidhara got Jambudweepa, Vapushmana Shelmahidweepa, Dyutimana Kromchadweepa, Medhatithi Plakshadweepa, Bhavya Shakadweepa, Savana Pushkardweepa and Jyotishmana Kushdweepa. King Agnidhara had nine sons: Nabhi, Kuinpurusha, Hevritla, Ramya, Shashtha, Hiranvana, Hari, Kunu and Bhadvashva. Jambudweep was further divided by Agnidhara among these sons. Nabhi got the part which later came to be renowned as Bharatavarsha.

Nabhi had a son called Rishabha who had a hundred sons, the eldest one was Bharata. It is claimed that Bharatavarsha acquired this name after this Bharata's name.

The Geographical Delineation

As we know the earth was divided into seven dweepa or continents called Jambu, Shalmali, Krouncha, Plaksha, Shaka, Pushkara and Kusha. These seven chunks of the land were surrounded by seven oceans called Lavana, Ikshu, Sura, Sarpi, Dadhi, Dugdha and Jaka. Jambudweepa is right in the middle and in the middle of Jambudweepa is the golden-coloured Mount Menu. The Purana claims that if the earth were to be a lotus flower, Mount Menu would be the stamen.

Immediately south of Mount Menu ties Bharatavarsha, then Kimpurush varsha and lastly Harivarsha. Due month of Menu lies first Ramayana, then Hiranmaya and eventually the northern part of Kunvarsha. Mount Menu is actually in Ilavritavarsha. And on four sides of Mount Menu are four mountains. To the east of Mandara, to the south Gandhamadana, to the west Vipula and to the north Suparshva. This part of the world came to be known as Jambudweepa because it has a natural growth of abundant 'Jamuna' trees. Jamuna in Sanskrit is called Jamba. There are four beautiful lakes around Mount Menu which were named Anurodha, Mahabhadra, Asitoda and Manas. It is said that on the peak of Mount Menu is Brahamloka or abode of Brahma.

It is claimed that the river Ganga originated from the feet of Vishnu when his one foot happened to cover whole of Brahmaloka while measuring all the three worlds in conformity with the concission allowed by king Vali. At that time Lord Vishnu had appeared in his Vamana form. There this river flew around the moon and later on fell in Brahma's Lok. Then the main stream gots divided into four rivers called Sita, Alaknanda, Chaksu and Bhadra. Sita flew east-wards. Alaknanda south wards and Bhadra northwards. In Bharatavarsha Alaknanda gets further divided into seven rivers.

If earth is deemed to be a print, Mount Menu is its Kernal which is also called Swarga or heaven, the abode of Gods, Goddesses, Gandharvas, Yakshas as also Rakshasas, Daityas and Danavas with the latter three, always wanting to possess the total control of the realm. But Swarga has access to only for the righteous people; the sinners must stay out of it as their entry is forbidden.

It is apparent that Bharatavarsha came to be so named became it is mainly inhabited by sons or progeny of Bharata. This choicest piece of the earth has seven major mountains ranges called Mahendra, Malaya,

Sahya, Shuktimana Ritasha, Vindhya and Paripatra. The kirat or hunters dwell due east from India and the Yavanas due west. The rivers Shatadru and Chandrabhaga flow out of the Himalayas. The main rivers mentioned in the Vedas that issue from Mount Paripetre are these two while rivers Narmada and Surasa issue from Mount Vindhya.

As mentioned before, Jambudweepa is surrounded by the ocean named Lavana. Vishnu is the chosen deity in Jambudweepa while other gods in other dweepas. The chunk of Jambudweepa called Bharastvarsha is the best part of this region.

While descending Patals (underworlds) on the earth, it is said that there are seven such regions: Atala, Vitala, Nitala, Gabhastimana, Mahatala, Sutala and Patal. These regions are the abodes of the Danavas, Daityas, Yakshas and Nagas. Once the divine sage Narad happened to visit Patala and found it to be more beautiful than even the Swarga. It was a place full of jewels. During the days the source of light was sun without any trace of heat while during the nights moonbeans kept it lightened but had no trace of cold in them Patala is described to be full of forests and lakes. The inhabitants of this part of the world were beautiful clothes, nubbed scented paste on their bodies and loved music. It was Vishnu who stayed at the base of Patal supporting it in the form of a thousand headed snake called Sheshnaga.

Underneath the earth and the water lay several hills (naraka)[1] which constitute the kingdom that yama rules over. There are different narkas for different types of sinners. Those who are held for perjuring are consigned to the Raurava naraka. Those who kill cows go to Rodha. Those who drink wine, kill Brahmans or steal gold go to Shukara. Those who kill Kshatriyas and Vaishyas go to Tola. Those who treat their teachers wives badly go to Tapta Kunda[2]. Those who kill messengers sell woman or horses go to Taptaloha.[3] Those who don't treat their daughters and daughters in law go to Mahajvala.[4] Those who show

---

[1] These are the kind of punishments prescribed for various offences and crimes and figuratively came to be reckoned as realms.

[2,3,4] Literally meaning boiling pond, red hot iron and raging fire respectively which clearly shows them to be a form of punishment for the specified offences.

disrespect to their seniors or criticise the Vedas go to Lavan. Thieves are consigned to Vimohana. The Calumniators of the Vedas or Brahmans and those who hats their fathers go to Krimibhaksha.

Also, those who eat before their fathers, gods and guests go to Lalabhaksha and those who make deadly arrows go to Vedhaka. The makers of swords go to the hell called Vishasana. Adhomukha is the hell for those who indulge in astrology.[Since it is tentament to revealing the future before its actual happening it is considered a sin as it is an attempt to claim parity with god] Fathers who eat sweet and choicest snakes without first allowing their children or the Brahmanas to partake of the same go to Puyevah hell. This is also the 'narak' for Brahmans who keep cats, hens, goats, dogs or birds to make a living. Brahmans who make their living as actors or fishermen, poisoners and arsonists go to the 'narak' called Rudhirandhas. Destroyers of the village are consigned to the hell called Vaitarani. The filthy and unclean go to Krishna narak. Destroyers of the forest for no special reason go to Asipatravana. Keepers of sheep for making a living or the killers of deer go to the hell called Vanhijwala. Fathers who study under their sons go to the hill called Shivabhojana. The opponents of the system that divides the population among the four classes go to the hell called Niraya.

However, apart from those that have been listed above their are thousands of other. So are the sins apart from those that have been hinted above. In the 'narakas' or hells sinners are tortured ruthlessly; they are hung upside down. Once they have paid for their sins by passing the stipulated time is hell, they are born again. What species they should be born in is decided by their performance in the previous lives. The descending order of the species is the following; gods, religious people, human, animals birds, fish, worms, creepers trees and other inanimate objects. But if a sinner is genuinely repentful of the sin he or she has committed them his or her soul need not pass the sluence in the various hells. The best way to repent for the sins committed is to worship Vishnu devotedly.

Some Astronomy and Story of Jadabharat

The Sun exists many miles above the earth. Descending from the Sun-loke (the realm of the sun) comes several realms of the moon, the stars, Mercury, Venus, Mars, Jupiter, Saturn and the Saptarishi [the great Bear constillations] and the Loka (realm) of Dhruva. The Dhruva Loka (Pole Star) is deemed to be the center of the entire universe around which the stars move. Above it is Jana Loka (devotees realm) where in dwell Brahma's sons. Above Janaloka is Tapoloka (the realms realised by severe penance) wherein gods live. Satyaloka (the realm of truth) is above Tapoloka which is divided into two separate realms: Brahmaloka and Vaikunthaloka of respectively Brahma and Vishnu.

Those that stay unaffected by the dissolution occurring at the end of each cycle of creation are the ones that inhabit Dhruvaloka, Janaloka, Tapoloka. But those three realms that stay below them are destroyed by Pralaya. The first of these lokas (realms) is of course the earth called the Bhurloka. The next realm a little higher to it is Bhuvarloka which is the abode of the sages and seers. Above this is the region called Svarloka covering Dhruvaloka to the realm of the sun? This way there are in all seven realms or gredations of the realms attained by various performances.

As a matter of fact, there are in all fourteen levels of reckoning by this Purana, the seven lokas and seven patals. They together are called fourteen Bhuvans. The whole universe is made of fourteen Bhuvans which are further categorized in three major levels of the realms (called three lokas). These Bhuvans remain covered by darkness from all sides which itself is covered by water. Water is surrounded by fire. Wind lies beyond fire and beyond fire is the sky. This way the entire universe is made of five elements, the sky, fire, water wind and the earth.

The Jadabharat Tale

As mentioned before, many years ago there ruled a powerful king called Bharat. His father's name was Rishabha who used to live in a place called Shalagrama. He was an ardent devotee of Lord Vishnu in whose devotion he was engrossed all the time. He was a strong believer in the cult of non-violence which he preached and practice in his life.

Once when Bharat had gone to take bath in a river, a deer had also come there to drink water there. While the deer was drinking water there was heard a terrible roar of a lion. In panic the deer gave a frightening leap and gave an untimely birth. But unprotected the baby deer fell into water. So frightened had the she-deer became that she died as a result of that leap. Bharat felt pity and rescued the baby deer from the water. He took the deer lying to the hermitage. Every day the king would lovingly feed the baby and slowly the deer grew bigger. It wandered around the hermitage and at times even out of it, but returned quickly as it was frightened of the beasts like tigers and lions. As it grew older, the deer would leave the ashrama (hermitage) in the mornings and return in the evenings.

Meanwhile, in the process of recovering that deer up, Bharat grew very attached to that deer and forgot everything else. He had given up his kingdom, his sons, his friends and had forgotten them all. If the deer was late in returning to the Ashrama he would worry that it might have been eaten up by a wolf or a tiger. He could forget everything else in the world but not the deer. Only when the deer returned safe and sound that he would be happy. So much so that in his infatuation to the deer he even forget about Vishnu, the Supreme Lord.

Many years elapsed this way. Bharat died watching the deer and thinking of it. Since the last thought in his mind centered on the deer at the time of his death, he himself was born as a deer in his next life. The only difference was that he was born as a JATISMARA deer — that is a deer that remembered the incidents of his past life. Since his memory had been intact, no sooner he was born as a deer than he left his deer-mother and came again to Shalagrama. He lived on dry leaves and grass and eventually died. Subsequently he was born as a JATISMARA Brahman. In this life he was truly learned and very much versed in all Shastras or scriptures.

Having attained the Supreme knowledge, he saw no point in reading the Vedas or in doing any work. He remained lost in his own world, and spoke as little as possible. He was totally unconcerned about his clothes and body. He never cleaned his teeth. His clothes always remained filthy. Owing to his these habits people treated him very badly. [Since he thought with interaction with people was an obstacle in his attaining] supreme knowledge, he pretended to be slightly mad to ward off the people from coming close. Also, he moved very little and mostly remained stationed at a place. His these practices made him acquire the title Jadabharat (the inimmobile Bharata). He also never cared for his food and ate whatever was available. Since he never objected to anything he was also yoked as a bullock by his inconsiderate brothers and nephews. When his father, died they offered only the 'Uchchishtha' food i.e., a food which was rejected by all.

Closeby the place Jadabharata lived at was also living the renowned sage Kapila. He had an ashrama (hermitage) on the banks of the river called Ikshumati. One day the king of Sanbhira happened to come close to the Ashrama to learn wisdom from the sage. As he reached close he needed the palanquin bearers. Though he had his servant they needed one more person. Eventually they found Jadabharata. Jadabharata bore the palanquin along with the other servants. But he walked slowly which made the movement of the palanquin turbulent as other servants could move fast. When the king scolded other palanquin bearers they blamed Jadabharat for the problem.

Why can't you move with others?" asked the king with scorn. "Can't you bear even this little burden? You look quite strong to me?

Jadabharat replied with marked non-challenge: "Neither I have borne your palanquin nor I'm. tired or strong."

The king found his reply quite strange: "I can see that you're strong.

I can also see that you are carrying my palanquin on your shoulders. So it is quite normal to feel a little tired. Why then you deny this? "Who am I or who are you?" began Jadabharat in his typical way. "What you have seen is my body and your body. I am not my body and nor you are your body. In fact what we really are is represented by the existence of our 'Atman'. And my atman is neither strong nor tired, nor it is carrying your palanquin on its shoulders!"

Jadabharat kept quiet after saying so. But the king got down from the palanquin and fell at Jadabharat's feet. He, now, wanted to know who Bharat really was, for such words of wisdom couldn't have been uttered by an ordinary man. Then Jadabharat enlightened him about the 'atman'. "Atman is never destroyed and it takes up different bodies from one life to another. This is called Jivatma. In addition, there is 'Paramatman' (the Supreme Soul). That is Lord Vishnu who permeates every bit of this creation. In fact Paramatma and Jivatman are the same. He who has realised this is a truly wise person. It is 'maya' or illusion which makes any distinction between Jivatman and Paramatman".

Mightily impressed the king honoured Jadabharat with a variety of ways. However, Jadabharat remained quite indifferent to them. Neverthless, he told the king a story.

Eons ago Brahma had a son known as Ribhu. He was a very learned one and he had a disciple called Nidagha, the son of Pulastiya. Both of them lived on the bank of the river called Devika, near a city known as Viranagar. While living there Ribhu realised that Nidagaha was still not ready enough to receive the supreme knowledge. In order to make him wiser he sent his pupil to live in the city while he himself continued to dwell in the forest.

After many days, One day Ribhu decided to pay Nidagha visit to ascertain as to how he was getting on. Seeing the teacher at his door Ribhu washed his hands and feet and offered him food.

"Please have some food, Sir!" Nidagha requested his guru.

"What have you got to eat?" asked Ribhu.

"Is it clean enough to be eaten by me."

"Yes Sir," replied Nidagha: "I have rice and cereals, fruit and sweets."

"But it doesn't appear clean to me", said Ribhu "I won't have them. Make some rice pudding, curds and wine for my consumption."

Nidagha, who was married, then asked his wife to prepare the desired fruit. The food was prepared according to the guests' choice and Ribhu had his fill.

Nidagha, then asked: "Are you content now?" When are you going and what was the purpose of your visit to my place?

Ribhu told him: "The hungry become content after eating food. But I wasn't hungry. Hence the question is irrelevant that I should have felt contented after eating food. Why ask me this silly question? I am not the body which feels hungry. Then you asked me where I was going and why did I come here. These are again meaningless question since what am I is all atman which is everywhere. Hence it cannot come or go. In fact I am not really what I appear to you. Nor are you what I see you to be. I simply had the food to see your reaction. Since all food is made of the five basic elements there is no difference in its taste to me. Learn this as this is the essence of all knowledge.

Getting this enlightened sermon Nidagha bowed his head and said now his all illusions stood dispelled and destroyed. Then Ribhu left to visit again after a gap of 1000 years. This time he found Nidagha living out side the city, eating grass and straw. He also ceased meeting others and became indifferent to his physical needs. Consequently, he had become very frail and thin. This time again Ribhu gave him a lesson on true knowledge which averred on detecting no difference between the atmana and Paramatman.

Concluding his narrative Bharata (Jadabharat) said that this was the knowledge that the king should aspire to acquire. The sky might appear blue or red some times but it didn't change the basic truth about it. Only those trapped in illusion distinguished between the 'atmana' and 'paramatman'. The whole world is instinct with one existence that is Atman or Paramatma who none other but Lord Vishnu.

The Manvantaras and The Vedvyasas

One cycle of creation and destruction is called Manavantara though literally this term in Sanskrit means 'the difference between the two consecutive Manus. A Manu is the ruler of each Manvantra. The Purana claims that there have been six Manvantaras thus far and the name of the Manu in each Manvantar are Swayambhuva. Svarochasha, Outtami, Tamasa, Raivata and Chakshusha, Vaivaswat. The son of the son rules over the present and seventh Manvantara called Shraddha. Each Manvantara has its well-defined gods and rishis (the seers). The Adityas (the sons of Aditi, the gods' mother) are the gods of the present Manvantara. Apart from them also adorable are the Randvas. Purandara is the Indra (chief of the gods) in this Manvantar. The seven rishis that command maximum respect in this epoch are Vashistha, Kashyapa, Atri, Jamadagni, Gautama, Vishwamitra and Bharadwaja.

Including the present one seven Manvantars have shown their presence and seven more are yet to come. The Manu of the Shraddha Manvantar — the present one — had nine very religious sons known as Ikshavaku, Nriga, Dhristha, Sharyati, Narishyant, Nabhag, Arishtha, Karusha and Prishadhra.

All these seven Manvantaras had the Supreme Lord Vishnu as their ultimate deity. In fact the ruler and creator of whole universe is none else but Vishnu in his myriad forms.

The Birth of Yama and Yami

Vishwakarma had a daughter named Sangya who was married to Surya, the sun. Their children were Manu, Yama and Yami. After some time, Sangya found that she could no longer bear the brilliance of her husband. So she created a woman known as Chhaya who looked exactly like her.[1] Having left Chhaya to look after her husband, she went off to meditate in a forest. Surya or the sun had no idea of this replacement and he still thought Chhaya to be Sangya. The Surya and Chhaya had two sons called Shaneischara (Saturns) and Savarni Manu and a daughter called Tapti.

One day when Chhaya found Yama not obeying her command she became very angry and cursed Yama. This curse made both Yama and Surya convinced that this woman could not be Sangya and must be someone else for mothers are not likely to curse their kids so casually. Upon further enquiry Chhaya told them the real story behind her replacement. When Surya learnt about Sangya performing penance (tapasya) in a forest in the form of a mare, he repaired to the spot after adopting the form of a horse. Reaching there he joined his wife again. While in the horse species they had three sons. The two Ashvini Kumars and one called Raivanta. After this, Surya escorted Sangya back to his realm. Realising his daughter's problems of her incapability of facing the sun's (Surya's) brilliance's, Vishwakarma tried his best to reduced it but could manage to reduce it by eighth part only. Falling on the earth subsequently, the eighth part became, the source of the creation of Lord Shankar's Trishool, the Viman (flying vehicle) of Kubera called Pushpaka, the Shakti (a lance) of Kartikeya and many other divine weapon's creation. Manu, the son of Chhaya was almost like Sangya's son. Manu and hence he earned the titles Savarni. Savarni would be the Manu of the eighth Manvantara and Indra would be Vali, the son of Virochan. The names of the Manu, of the Manvantar that would follow would be Dakshasavarni (9th), Brahmasavarni (10th). Dharamasavarni (11th), Savarna (12th), Rouchya (13th) and Bhautya (14th).

---

[1] This is an allegorical interpretation of the sunlight and shadow since Chhaya means shadow.

Since the Vedas are also destroyed at the end of every Manvantara, the respective Manu rewrites the sacred Vedas and other Shastras. As already declared in each Manvantar, Manu, the seven rishis. Indra and gods, and kings are created afresh. One cycle of 14 Manvantars go to make one Kalpa And at the end of a Kalpa dawns Brahma's night. During that (Brahma's night) Vishnu in his Brahma form sleeps on the water overwhelming all the universe.

Only at the termination of such grand night, owing to Supreme god's wish, gets created the universe (Srishti) afresh. Hence Manu, Devatas (gods) Indra and Manu's progeny are instinct with only one Existences, Lord Vishnu.

Lord Shreenarayan (Vishnu) incarnates Himself in every Yug in his different forms. In Satyayug He disseminates knowledge in the form of Kapil in the First (Satya) Yug. In the Second Age — i.e., Treta He incarnets Himself as kings to slay the wicked and protect the noble. In every Dwapar Yug. He incarnates as Vedvyas to edit the Vedas and add further accumulated knowledge. In Kalikaal (Kaliyug) He incarnates as Kalki to establish again the rule of law and righteous conduct.

Vedavyas[2]

Vedavyas is actually a title. In each age Vishnu in his form of Vedavyas divides the entire knowledge acquired into various Vedas. This massive editing and vetting takes place in every Dwapar age. [Perhaps the earlier demarcation goes topsy-turvy by this time, hence the need after two Ages: Satya Yuga and Treta}. In the present Manvantar whose Manu is Vaivasvata the Vedas have already under gone 28 divisions by the Vedavyasses of even number. The names of these Vedavyas are given below in the Chronological order.

Swayambhuva, Prajapati, Ushana, Brishaspati', Savita, Mrityu, Indra, Vashishtha, Saraswata, Tridhama, Trivrisha, Bharadwaj Antariksha, Vakri, Trayaruna, Dhananjaya, Kritanjaya, Rinanjaya, Bharadwaj (PerhapsII), Gautama, Haryatma, Vena, Trinarindu, Riksha,

---

[2]The literal meaning of this term is that he who can fathom the Vedas as a diameter (Vyas) fathoms the circle.

Shaktri, Parashara, Jatukarna, and Krishna Dweipayana.[3] The Vishnu purana claims that the next Vedavyas will be Ashwathama.[4]

Each Vyas compiles the knowledge into the category of the Vedas according to his own comprehension of the knowledge of his Age, accrued to man till that particular Manvantar.

In the beginning of the creation the Vedas had, together, one lakh shlokas. In the 28th Dwapar Krishna Dweipayan Vyas divided the whole knowledge, in conformity with the style adopted by the earlier Vyasas, into four categories and initiated four scholars to study them. Paila became well versed in the Rig-Veda, Vaishampayan in Yajur-Veda, Jaimini in Sam Veda and Sumantu in Atharva-Veda. Romharshan, belonging to the Sootajati (the class that drove the chariots) was chosen for mastering the Purana and Itihas. It is from the Vedas that the ten famous sacrifices (yagyas) originate.

Yagyavalkya Story

The Vyas taught Yajurveda dividing it into 27 sections and gave this knowledge to his 27 disciples. Among those 27 disciples, one of them was the son of Brahmarata, called Yagyavalkya.

Once upon a time, the famous rishis decided that they would gather and have the religious discourse to finally edit the knowledge that was made available to them. They also decided that who ever did not come to this gathering would after a period of seven days commit the crime of killing a brahmana [i.e., Not coming to this gathering for a period of one week would be tentamount to the negligent's committing a crime as severe as killing a brahmana].

All the sages duly came to this gathering barring Vaishampayana. After seven days. Vaishampayan really stepped on his nephew and killed him accidently. Since this was a terrible sin it had to be atoned for.

Whereupon Vaishampayana called his all disciples together and said: "I have committed the crime of killing a brahmana. Please arrange for a sacrifice so that I might atone for this deadly sin."

---

[3]Named so because he was born in a dweep or an island. Hence the term Dweipayan.
[4]He is one of the seven immortals according to the Hindu belief.

Hearing this Yagyavalkya said rather pompously: "There is no need to bother other disciples for this. They don't have much power I will arrange for the entire sacrificial ceremony myself."

Vaishampayan was angry hearing this arrogant assertion. You have insulted the other disciples by making this pompous statement, Yagyavalkya. The punishment is: return to me all that you have acquired from me. Every bit of the knowledge. I don't need a disciple like you."

Yagyavalkya was still delinquint. He said: "I said what I did because I have regard for you. The fact is I, too, don't need teacher like you. Here is all that I have learnt from you. I am returning it."

It is said that Yagyavalkya, there and then puked out the entire learning he had received in the form of Yajurveda. The other disciples ate it up in the form of birds called Titar (a form of patridges). That is the reason why this branch of The Yajurveda is called Taittariya after the name of the bird Titar.

However Yagyavalkya wasn't satisfied after getting rid of the knowledge he had acquired from Vaisham-Payana and still wanted to learn Yajurveda. So with this desire he began to pray to the sun. Propitation duly the sun appeared before him in the form of horse and taught him those branches of the Yajurveda which even Vaishampayana was ignorant about.

The Creation of the Puranas

Puranas literally mean an account of the past. Hence can be loosely translated as 'history'. The Vishnu Purana describes as to how they came to be written. It says that the original text, 'Purana Samhita' was taught by Vedavyas to his disciple Romaharshana also called Lomaharshana, as hinted before Romaharshana had six disciples: Sumati, Agnivarchaha, Mitrayu, Shamshapyana, Akritaverna and Savarni. Each of these disciples composed of a Purana on the basis of Purana Samhita. In fact this Puranas Samhita is also the basis on which this Vishnu Purana had been written. It was written after Padma Purana which describes the glories of Lord Vishnu.

The Vedvyas had divided all the Purana under 18 headings. They are:

1. Brahma Purana

2. Padma Purana
3. Vishnu Purana
4. Shiv Purana
5. Bhagawata Purana
6. Narada Purana
7. Markandeya Purana
8. Agni Purana
9. Bhavishyata Purana
10. Brahma — Vaivarta Purana
11. Linga Purana
12. Varaha Purana
13. Skanda Purana
14. Vamana Purana
15. Koorma Purana
16. Matsya Purana
17. Garuda Purana
18. Brahmanda Purana

Some sages have also created sub-sections of these Puranas which all contain the details of origin of life on this planet.

According to Sanatana Dharma there are fourteen types of knowledge (Vidya). The four Vedas, six Vedangas, Mimansa, Nyaya, the Puranas and the Dharma-shashtras constitute these 14 main branches of Vidya. Added to these, later on was Ayurveda, Dhanurveda, Sangeeta-Veda and Arthshashtra.

This faith recognizes three categories of the rishis (noble learned souls): Brahma-rishis, Devarishis and Rajarishis which can be respectively rendered as the rishis having the knowledge of the Supreme, the rishis having the knowledge of the Divine and the rishis having the knowledge of the royalty.

Yama

Having learnt about all knowledge and its varied classifications. Maitreya ji asked Parashar sage if with all this knowledge one could get over the bondage of death. Where upon Parashar narrate him a story which was recounted by Bhishma, the grandsire of Mahabharata fame while answering a question asked by Nakul, the fourth Pandava. Bhishma said: "Once I had a friend, a Brahman who belonged to Kalingadesh. Once he happened to meet a Jatismara sage, Who told the Brahman some facts about the latter's future which subsequently was found to be very correct. The Brahman developed great reverence for that sage's capacity to see through so deep into one's future. Then he also asked few more questions which further deepened his faith in the sage. Then he asked sage if there could be any means by which one could avoid facing the messengers of the death god. Then he narrated a dialogues that had taken place between the death god and his messengers. The death-god or yama instructed his messengers this way: "None of you should ever dare trouble the devotees of Lord Vishnu. Because he is my Lord also and it is at his behest that I keep the account of the beings' age and death, their sins and merits which are the parameters to ascertain the beings, eventual abode in which realm. So you should also respect all the Vishnu-devotees. You can over-power only those that are indifferent to Vishnu. The moral of this story is that no matter, how-learned one be, if one has, no faith in Lord Vishnu one can't attain immortality.

The Four Classes, The Four Stages, Sanskaras and The Mayamoha Tale

The ideal way of following Vishnu is to follow the law of the four classes (Varna) and the law of the four stages (ashramas) as laid down in the Shashtras created at Lord Vishnu's behest. Those who do not deviate from what is laid down for their class, those who make no distinctions between the friends and the foes since all are Vishnu's creation; those who are not thieves; those who adhere to the truth and non-violence, those whose heart is guiltless and free from anger are the real devotees of Lord Vishnu.

The four classes in any society are represented by the Brahmanas, Kshatriyas, Vaishyas and Shudras. The Shashtras enjoin upon Brahman as to give alms, worship the gods through sacrifices and study the Vedas. They should treat all living beings well and not harm anyone by word and deed. The most important wealth that a Brahman can have is to have friendship with all.

The Shashtras ask Kshatriyas to donate to Brahman as much as the fulfil their daily needs, study Shashtras with the Brahmans' guidance, perform sacrifice to Vishnu. A Kshatriyas foremost duty is to bear arms and protect the earth. He is the king and his duties are to punish the evil and protect the good so that righteousness prevails. The Vaishyas are to do trade, agriculture, animal husbandry. In addition, they should study, donate alms and perform sacrifice. The Shudra's duty is to serve classes and leisure their comfort. In case it is impossible to make a living through this, the Shudras may earn where withal through trade or handicrafts and other the such means.

However, besides the special duties, the Shastras also enjoin certain common duties to all classes. Everyone of them should be kind to all; they must ensure their physical cleanliness, be truthful and friendly to all with enough capacity to bear hardships and adversity. In case there be a possibility of a Brahman unable to make a living through the means that are laid down, he can take up arms and perform the duties of a Kshatriyas. Or, he can take up agriculture, animal, husbandry or trade. In the distressing conditions a Kshatriyas may also take up agriculture, animal husbandry or trade. However a Brahman or a Kshatriya should never stoop down to as low as to take up the duties of a Shudra. This can only be allowed in the situation of the Apaddharma (in absolutely distressing conditions) when there be no other alternative. It is the duty of every member of the society to see that the clearly defined duties do not get mixed up for then it would be anarchy.

Among the four stages of life called 'ashramas' the first one is 'brahmacharya' which can be loosely rendered as celibate student hood. Roughly stretching to about one fourth of the total span of human life, this is the period when one should assimilates from world all the knowledge that is possible. It is in this stage that the boy after he has been invested with his sacred thread, should be sent to his teacher's house or school for learning the Vedas and other knowledge. There he should lead a clean life and pay attention to his ritual. In this period he should serve his guru devotedly and study the Vedas. Every morning and evening — before the sun rise and after the sun-set respectively — he should say his prayers dedicated to the sun and the fire and how to his teacher after the prayers are over. The disciple (the 'batuk' or student) should sit after his guru has sat and follow whatever his guru says. Bringing flowers every morning to his guru, supplying water and helping the guru in his domestic chores is also a part of the student's duty during this first stage. Eventually the Shishya will have learnt the Vedas and attained knowledge. Completing his education the Shishya (disciple) must pay to his guru his fees called Guru Dakshina. It is only after the guru permits him that he will step in the next ashrams — the ashrams of family life or grihastha. Then he will assume his worldly duties staying at home.

This ashram starts with boy getting married and choosing a proper living. Such a person has to serve gods through sacrifices, guests through food, rishis through reading the Vedas, Brahma through having children and the entire world through truthfulness. In many ways the 'Grahastha Ashrama' is held superior to the others. The Brahmanas and those who follow Brahmacharya may have to survive on alms they receive. It is the 'Grihasthas or the person having attained this ashram who provide alms to the students and Brahmans. When guests arrive, the householder will offer whatever he can in the nature of food, seats and beds. If a guest goes away dissatisfied, he takes away the householder's 'Punya' (accumulated merit) and leaves his son with his hosts. That is why a guest should be always treated properly and nothing that he desires should be refused.

This ashrama ends when a person has discharged his worldly duties and enjoyed all pleasure of life. After this ashram he may proceed to the Vanaprashtha Ashram or the ashram of dwelling (or going towards) forest. In fact this is the stage when he should start detaching himself from his worldy bonds although he can take along his wife with him. Should she desire she can also stay back with her sons? In the forest he should live on fruits and roots and leaves sleep on the ground. During this stage all cosmetics care of his body should be discontinued, including even cutting his hair occasionally or shaving his beard. He should worship the gods, tend to guests and give alms to the needy as much as he possibly can. In this stage the person's main occupation should be worship. He must try to become as much detached from the world as possible and live close to nature.

The final stage in Sannyas Ashrama. This is the stage when he should have a totally dispassionate view of the entire creation. One enters this stage when he can give up all the worldly bonds and became equi distant[1] with all the animate inanimate objects of the world. This

---

[1]Sannyas is the term which means (sam) even (+ nyas) placement. So literally this means some one who is having no prejudice or prediliction for any person place or thing.

is the stage when a person becomes evenly friendly with everything in the creation. He should have no particular attachment to anything. He should not harm anyone in any way. He will live all alone and perform yogic exercise i.e., the exercises that unite man with god. He should never stay in a village for more than one night at a time and in a city for more than five nights at a time. A Sanyasi or hermit should beg for his food and shouldn't have food cooked by himself. Moreover, he will come to a house for begging food only when everyone in the house has eaten to his fill. His share could be only the leftover food items. This is the stage which prepares the person for his final release.

Samskars or the Rituals Enjoined for the Native

Having narrated the various class divisions and stages Parashar sage, while quoting the dialogue that took place between Sagar and Aurva, he mentioned about the various rituals that must be observed for every human being.

At the occasion of the son's birth the father must perform a thanks-giving ceremony (Shraddha) to god for the continuation of his lineage. This type of Shraddha is called Abhyudaya Shraddha in which two Brahmans should be fed and then after offering oblations to his aguatis and family divinities he should observe the ritual of the Pinda-daan[2]. On the Tenth Day the new arrival should be given a name. His name must have some divinity's name in the beginning (like Krishna, Ram etc.) a middle name followed by his caste identification.

At the age of eight years the sacred thread (Yagyopaveeta) ceremony of the son should be performed. Then after he should be sent to some school. When he has completed he should be married. The age of the bride should be three fourth of that of the groom.

Telling about the kinds of marriage Aurva told that there were eight kinds of marriages: Brahm, Daiva, Aarsha, Prajapaatya, Asura (demniac), Gandharva, Rakshasa and Pishaacha Marriage. After marriage the son should settle in family life in conformity with his family

---

[2]Customary oblation of cooked rice offered to the manes on the especial occasion like the day of Shraddha etc.

traditions. Unless a father has his son's marriage consummated he doesn't earn any merit either in this world or in the next.

The ideal routine of a family man should be following. An intelligent person must get up early in the morning. Then he should go to jungle or some lovely spot to evacuate his bowels. While defecating he must keep his head covered and shouldn't speak. This should be followed by proper washing of hands and feet and then of the teeth. After taking bath he should say his prayers and pay his regards to his ancestors and the sages. If there be any respectable person or Brahman available in the house, the householder must feed him properly before himself taking food. He must ensure that while having his food, first he must have something sweet, then salty and in the last bitter or pungent edible. First he must have some liquid food then solid food and in the end again liquid food. If this order in taking food is followed one remains always healthy.

After having his food he should go for earning his living. In the evening when he returns he must wash his hands and feet and then say his evening prayers before partaking of his evening meal.

He must complete with his wife on the given auspicious days but never during her periods, illness or pregnancy. He shouldn't force his wife to copulate. Copulating with over-filled or empty stomach is bad for the system. Copulation is also prohibited on 14th and 8th lunar days as also on full moon days; in the morning and evening; when one has one's bowels' or bladder full, in guru's ashrama or holy place; beneath a trees in the lunar month of Chaitra (15th March to 15th April) or at any public place. Observing this rule keeps one free of sexual or other diseases.

A good householder should never steal, tell a lie, or utter what is unpleasant to others. He should never describe others faults and must be free of jealousy for others. He must keep a distance between him and wicked beings. He should never enter a burning house or limb to the top of a tree. While yawning, not covering one's mouth is unmannerly. He should be careful of stepping on the shadows of gods and flags and those who should be worshipped.

A good householder does not leave his house before bowing to a religious object, a flower, a jewel; clarified butter (ghee) or respectful persons. When travelling by night he must keep a stick in his hands. He should always use an umbrella while going in the sun. He should always tell truth but when the truth appears to harm anyone, he should keep quiet.

When a householder dies, his body should be bathed and garlanded. The dead body must always be burnt out side the village.[3] For a brahmana the Shraddha ceremony takes place after ten days; for a Kshatriya after twelve days and for Vaishya 15 days. The Shudras get cleand of the defilement caused by death (Ashaucha) after a full month of the death. During the period of Ashaucha no auspicious ceremony should be performed. Even ritual worship and alms giving also remain suspended during this period. When this period is over, according to one's capacity three, five, seven or nine Brahmans should be ceremonially fed. After they have been fed, for the satisfaction of the spirit of the departed person, a few personal belongings of the departed soul-placed upon a mat made of the Kushagrass and touched by water, weapon, a whip and a stick should be donated to the Brahmans who have been fed. After this on every moonless day for a full year subsequently a noble Brahman should be fed after completing the Pinda-daan. These ceremonies should be performed only by the descendants of the same family to which the departed soul belonged — like the departed person's son, grandson, brother or his son-etc.

In case on the moonless day of the lunar month of Magh (Mid-December to Mid January) the constellations of Shatbhisha [Lambda-Aquarius] be rising, that would constitute an ideal moment for the propitiation of the soul of departed person. Dhanishtha's[4] ascending on that very day becomes all the more auspicious for the propitiation of the departed soul since this ceremony on that occasion is behind to satisfy the soul for a period of 10,000 years. The oblations offered to the departed soul on the bank of some holy river like the Ganga, Jamuna, Satluj, Vyas or Gomti adds to the merit of the departed soul to

---

[3]His bones should be picked on the fourth day of the cremation.

[4]Dhanishtha or Beta Delphinum. 1. Some version claim meat preparations are the best dish to be offered to his guest at this ceremony.

facilitate its release from the cycle of births and deaths. The departed ancestors always desire their soul's propitiation this way by their legal descendants.

The Aurva sage further told that for the performance of the Shraddha ceremony, the chosen Brahman must be well versed in the Vedas. He should not be indulging in the vices of any kind and must not be of vile nature. While feeding the Brahmana reverentially the host must deem his departed ancestor's presence in that Brahmana.

Any performance of the Shraddha ceremony in the city of Gaya accrues additional merit to the credit of the departed soul. But the care should be taken that the food prepared on this occasion must not be seen by an impotent person, a perish, a sinner or a lady passing through her menstruation period.

A good family man should always wear clean clothes. He should be sweet-tongued person with aversion to speaking lies. He must have noble feelings for those who are by nature holy and god-fearing. Cleaning the nose before all, coughing with mouth open, laughing like hilariously, farting with a loud noise, munching the hair of the beard or the moustaches, writing on the earth surface, beholding a naked woman of some other man, seeing the rising or the setting son, sleeping in a crematorium ground, at a public place, beneath the tree of Chaitya, devoting a long time in physical exercises, copulating with wife while taking bath, sleeping without clothes, sneezing or spitting while worshipping the deities are some of the ill-mannerly practices which a good house holder should never indulge in.

The Tale of Mayamoha

Eons ago there ensued a war between the demons and the good which lasted for about a year. The war ended when some Daitya (demons) called 'Hrada' defeated the divinities. Trounced the gods fled to the northern shores of an ocean and there they started to pray Lord Vishnu. Hearing their succour Lord Vishnu appeared before them. To help them He created there and then a being called Mayamoha[5] out of

---

[5]Literally infatuation due to the divine spell of illusion.

66

his own body. Led by Mayamoha, the gods went ahead to teach the demons a bitter lesson and settle their scores with them.

At that time the Asuras (demon) were performing sacrifice on the banks of the river Narmada. Mayamoha appeared before them dressed in leaves and with a shaven head. He told them that the best way to attain what the demons were aspiring for was following the religion preached by his own self. The demons were persuaded by Mayamoha to leave the path of the Vedas. The 'Asuras' who adopted this new religion came to be known as 'Arhats'. Influenced by the new religion they began to Criticise the Vedas and the gods. They also despired all sacrificial practices and became averse to the brahmanas importance.

This way, when the gods eventually launched attack on the Arhat demons the latter had already deniated from the righteous path. Consequently the Asuras were easily trounced by the gods since the Asuras had already lost their moral force.

[The moral of this story is clear. God himself tests this devotees by creating illusions before them which take the latter away from the righteous path. Those who get swayed by this illusions get always defeated in life]

Those who criticise the path ordained by the Vedas are called 'Nagnas' [i.e, unclad by civilization] Even holding talks with such persons is damaging to one's reputation and values. Then Parachar recited a tale in this context.

The Tale of Shatadhanu and Shaivya

There ruled a king called Shatadhanu many years ago. He was an ardent devotee of Lord Vishnu. His wife Shaivya was also a very religious person. It was their daily ritual to go to the banks of the river Bhagirathi and offer their prayers to Lord Vishnu. So deeply were they devoted to Lord Vishnu's worship that they were not interested in any other pursuit. They were living happily engrossed in their worship to Lord Vishnu when a fraudulent teacher came to them. Since Shaivya detected that teacher to be not a nice being to talk to, she refused to hold any kind of dialogue with him but, as her bad luck would have, her husband, Shatadhanu granted the fraudulent teacher an audience. Some years later, Shatadhanu died and Shaivya also died with him, becoming Sati, on the funeral pyre.

As a consequence of Shatadhanu's talking to that fraudulent Veda-Caluminator, the king in the next life was born as a dog. And Shavya was born as a 'Jatismara' daughter to the king of Kashi. When the king of Kashi wished to get his daughter married off, Shaivya refused. She had learnt that her husband had been born as a dog and was living in the city of Vidisha. So she went there and met the dog. She gave it good food to eat. The dog only kept on wagging his tails. At this, Shaivya felt quite ashamed and crest fallen. Then she kept on reminding the dog of its earlier life.

At last the dog had its memory of the previous life revived. Realising its great fall in species in this life the dog was very sad. It left the city and climbed a mountain peak. From there it threw itself down on the desert and died.

This time (in the second life after dog's species) it was born as a jackal. Shavya again traced him and met the jackal at the mountain named Kolahala. She reminded the jackal of its earlier life. Thus reminded, the jackal died in the forest and was born as a wolf. Shaivya traced the wolf again died remined of its earlier life. Mortified the wolf died soon. Next time it was reborn as a vulture. Shaviya went to meet it. This time, after the death of the vulture, Shatadhanu was born as a crow. In the next life the crow was born as a peacock. Shaivya again traced it and became friendly with this peacock.

It was around that time that King Janaka was performing an 'Ashwamedha' sacrifice. The peacock happened to have bath at the time of the sacrifice Shaivya also happened to be there and she again reminded the peacock of its former life. It died. It was now born as the son of Janaka and Shaivya agreed to marry him. After Janaka died, his son became the ruler of the kingdom of Videha. In this life Shatadhanu performed many sacrifices and gave many alms. He had several sons and ruled the kingdom and the earth well. When he died, Shaivya again died with him on the funeral pyre. Hushed and wife then repaired to heaven.

The story illustrates the consequence of speaking to the fraudulent ('naked') person who despise Vedas and tried on the evil path. Such being go direct to hell of the worst kind.

Various Dynasties from Manu

Detecting Maitreya ji's curiosity to known about the various dynasties of mankind, the sage Parashar said:"In the beginning of creation, Vishnu in his form of Brahma came out of 'Brahmanda' (the Golden Egg which is believed to be the origin of the universe). From Brahma's fingers was born Daksha Prajapati. Daksha's daughter was Aditi. Aditi's son was Surya and Surya's son was Manu. With the intention of getting a son he prayed to Maitra Varuna. He performed a Yagya for this purpose, and out emerged from the holy fire a daughter Ila. But since Manu had really desired a son, in a twice, Ila got converted into a man called Sudyumna, subsequently.

Meanwhile, Chandra had a son called Buddha. One day while wandering around Buddha's Ashram as the girl Ila; Buddha fell for her and married her. They had a son called Puroorva. After Puroorva's birth, Ila performed great sacrifice to have herself converted into a man, Sudyumna. When she became the man Sudyumna, in the changed from, Sudyumna had three sons called Utkala, Gaya and Vinata.

Then following Sage Vashishtha's orders Manu made Sudyumna the ruler of Pratishtanpur. Then after Sudyumna entruted the rulership to Puroorva when the latter came of age. Purvoorva had many Kshatriya sons who spread in many directions to establish their control.

Further down in this dynasty was born a king called Marutta. Marutta performed a wonderful Yagya. That was performed with such grandeur that no Yagya of that class was performed ever since. Every artich used in the ceremony was made of gold. Indra drank a lot of 'soma juice' and was fully satisfied. So were all the Brahmanas who performed the Yagya. Even the gods were asked to serve food in this Yagya which was ambrosial.

Further down in this very family there was a king called Sharyati? He had a daughter named Sukanya who was married to the renowned sage Chyavana. Meanwhile, Sharyati also had a son Revata. He had many sons — as many as hundred — and the eldest was Kakuddami. His daughter was Revati. Kakudami was not sure who should be the ideal groom for his daughter. In order to seek help he repaired to Brahmaloke to seek Brahma's advice. At the time he reached Brahma's loka he found the Gandharvas were singing. He sat down and listened attentively to their songs. When the musical session was over he asked Brahma whom he should get Revati married to.

What is your preferences?" Brahma asked although Kakudami named several kings whom he thought might be good husbands for Revati Brahma told him that while he was listening to the Gandharva's songs several thousand years had passed on earth. These kings whom he named and their sons and grandson — all were died. So much time had elapsed, the creator told Kakudami, that now even his (Kakudami's) capital Kushasthali was now a city called Dwaraka. And Vishnu as Baldeva had taken birth there". He should be the ideal husband for your daughter Revati, O King," concluded Brahma.

When Kakudami returned to earth he found men much reduced in size. They were much shorter than what they used to be. But his daughter, Revati, was as tall as before. But as Baldeva's marriage was fixed to Revati, he pulled Revati down to the right size before marrying him with the help of the plough which he always carried.

That of Ikshvaku Yuvanashva And Soubhari

Once upon a time Manu happened to sneeze, and out emerged from his nose a son called Ikshavaku. Ikshavaku had a son called Vikushi Once Ikshavaku wanted to perform the ceremony of Shraddha of his ancestors and he wanted special meat from the forest brought for this purpose. Vikushi killed many a deer for the ceremony and so he felt hungry and tired. In order to satisfy his hunger he ate a rabbit and brought the other meat to his father, who then offered the meat to Vashistha, the chief priest of the ceremony.

But Vashishtha objected, saying this meat was unclean." It appears your son has eaten himself the best meat (that of a rabbit) that he could procure."

Hearing this charge on his son Ikshavaku banished Vikushi although Vikushi did rule the kingdom after Ikshavaku's death. Vikushi had a brave son called Parjanya. The gods and the demons were engaged in a terrible war which remained indecisive for many years. Then the gods prayed to Vishnu and Vishnu told them that he would be born on earth as Parjanya and that under Parjanya's leadership the gods would be able to defeat the Asuras. When the gods heard about the advent of Parjanya, they requested him to lead their forces. Parjanya agreed to do this only if he could fight the war perched on Indra's shoulders. This Condition made Indra adopt, the form of a bull and Parjanya fought the war seated on that bull. The demons were then defeated. But from the word 'Kakut' which means shoulders, Parjanya also came to be known as 'Kakustha' which literally means the one seated on the shoulders.

Yuvanashva was Kakustha's most brilliant descendant. However, Yuvanashva did not have any son. So he persuaded the sages to perform a Yagya in order to make him get a son. Accordingly, the ceremony began and by the time it came to an end it was mid-night. The sages preserved the sacred water in a pot. It was to be given to Yuvanashav's wife early in the morning. She was supposed to get a strong son after drinking that water. But as the destiny would have it, Yuvanashva himself felt very thirsty in the late night and without caring for anything he drank that water by mistake. So a baby came into Yuvanashva's body and grew bigger and bigger. When the time came for the baby to be born, it burst out through the king's right side (rib cage) although the king survived the ordeal. But, now, the problem emerged as to who should be the baby's mother? Given the peculiar circumstances Indra gallantly argued to become the mother of the baby. He came forward and 'Man dhata' (I'll nurse it). This expression was used to name the son who became famous as Mandhata. Since Indra was nursing him he became full grown in the period of just one single day. He proved to be great ruler, reigning over the full earth — right from the point the sun rose to the point the sun set in.

It was during Mandhata's reign that a sage Soubhari completed a very difficult penance of living under water for 12 years. He used to keenly behold the king of fishes playing in the water with its children and grand children. This tempted Soubhari to pine for the stage where he could also marry and have children. But who should he marry to?

Mandhata, meanwhile, had fifty daughters. So Soubhari went to him with his desire of marriage. He requested the king to marry his one daughter off to him. But Mandhata was not willing, He found the body of the sage weak and sickly. But at the same time he also knew the sage's might. If he refused the sage was sure to curse him. In order to find an escape route, Mandhata said that his family custom was allowing the daughter to marry by choice. So they could marry only some one they linked and approved of Soubhari, however, realized that it was the king's play to avoid giving his daughter in marriage to Soubhari. At this, Soubhari requested the king to give him one chance to meet his daughters. In case any of them consented to marry him, he would marry only then. If all of them refused to marry him he would quietly leave the place without having his this desire fulfilled. Then he would not insist on his marriage.

Mandhata found it to be quiet a reasonable request, so he agreed for it. He was not aware of the sage Soubhari, hidden strength. As soon as the day of marriage came close, Soubhari transformed him into a very handsome man. He in fact, looked so handsome that all the 50 daughters of Mandhata expressed their desire to marry sage Soubhari. The result was that Soubhari married all the fifty daughters and he took them to his hermitage. Reaching there he summoned Vishkarma, the divine architect, to build 50 separate beautiful palace for his 50 wives. Each palace was to be endowed with a pleasure garden, beautiful beds and with a lake full of swans. Vishkarma did as he was told and in no time 50 incomparable jewelled palaces were built.

After a few months, Mandhata wished to find as to how his daughters were. He came to the sage's hermitage and joined 50 grand palaces close by. He entered one of the palaces and met one of his daughters there. "How are you, daughter? he asked.

'Wonderful !' she said: "I live in this beautiful palace. Look at the pleasure garden decorated with beautiful birds and the cool lake in their middle. I eat lovely food and wear choicest clothes. The only complaint I have is that my husband passes much time with me. This means that my other sisters might be deprived of his company!"

Amazed, Mandhata came out of the place and went inside another. To his great surprise he found his every daughter expressing almost their identical feelings. In fact with his Yogic powers, Soubhir had created fifty different forms of himself. Mandhata had never witnessed any thing like this before. Overwhelmed by Soubhir's spiritual might, he fell flat at the sage's feet and begged for forgiveness.

Soubhir produced hundred and fifty sons from those daughters of Mandhata. He was very much attached to all his sons. But he also realised that this kind of infatuation was going to create a big hurdle in his tapasya (devoted penance). This thought at once made him averse to worldly attachments since he realized the illusion he had been living with ever since he had seen that king of fishes living with his family. Immediately he left for the woods and devoted his rest of the life in the worship of Lord Vishnu.

That of Sages Mandhata's descendants were quite powerful and strong. Among them the most noteworthy was Purukutsa. He was very famous and brave.

Many ages ago the another world (Patal lok) was occupied by 60 million Mauneya Gandharvas. They drove away the Nag Devatas (a race that worshipped serpents as deites) and stole their jewels. The routed nagas prayed to Vishnu for deliverance. Propitiated by the genuineness of the feeling, Vishnu appeared before them and said. "I'd soon enter Purukutsa's body and make him destroy the Gandharvas. In order to invite Purukutsa to their world they sought the help of the river Narmada. Getting the invitation Purukutsa came there and in as twice destroyed all the Mauneya Gandharvas. The nagas were inmensly happy and they granted Narmada a boon: Who ever says" O Mother Narmada, protect me from the snakes poison as I chant your name every morning and evening" be never bitten by snakes.[1]

It was in the same dynasty that king Vahu was born, once having lost a war with some other kings the king retired to the forest with his two queens. There Vahu's wife was about to deliver a baby when his other queen gave the expected mother deadly poison out of jealousy since she thought that after the delivery the king might love his that wife more dearly. The result was that the baby did not come out but stayed inside the mother for seven years. King Vahu died in the hermitage of the sage Aurva. Then Vahu's wife also wished to die on the funeral pyre.

But the sage Aurva: "No, you can't Queen! What are you trying to do is sin. You are carrying a son who will be the bravest of the brave. He will be a great warrior; he will conquer many lands and perform many sacrifices. Don't kill him along with you on the funeral pyre."

Eventually the queen dropped the idea and the boy was born. Sagar was the name the child, child received from the sage. He also taught the boy the Vedas and various Shastras along with the martial arts. As he grew up Sagar wished to win back his father's lost kingdom. He not only defected the enemy kings but managed to conqueror the entire world. Sagar had two wives: Sumati and Keshini. They both prayed to sage Aurva that they might have sons. Aurva granted them the boon saying: "One of you will have only single son while the other as many as 60,000 sons." Keshini desired to have a single son whereas Sumati wanted 60,000 sons. And they eventually had their wishes fulfilled. Keshini had a single son whose name was Asmanjas. But all the sons of Sumati turned out to be quite evil. When they became more disturbing the gods went to the sage Kapila and asked him to rescue the world from these evil sons of Sagar.

Meanwhile, Sagar thought of performing an 'Ashwamedha Yagya' and having performed it he entrusted the responsibility of protecting the cousecrated horse to his 60,000 sons. While they were moving behind

---

[1]Narmadayei namah praatah, Narmadayei namah nishi Namoastu Narmade tubhyam trahi mam vish serpated II

the son, Indra stole the consecrated horse. His worry was lest Sagar should claim his position following the completion of the Ashwamedha Yagya. So Indra not only stole the horse but took it to the nether world and tied it to a pig in the sage Kapil's ashrama. The sage Kapila was busy performing his worship unmindful of the consecrated horse's presence before his Ashram.

Meanwhile the 60,000 sons of Sagar were panicky and searched for it frantically. Eventually trailing it down to the nether world. They found the horse wandering around the underworld and not far from the horse, they saw Kapila, the sage busy in his worship. Concluding that the sage must have stole their horse, they attacked the sage with their weapons. But a terrible fire issued forth from Kapila's eyes and reduced Sagar's sons to ashes.

While these tidings were taking place King Sagar was dead and replaced by his son Asmanjas who had a son called Anshuman. On learning his grand uncles having been reduced into ashes Anshuman was sent to fetch the horse. He reached Kapila's Ashrama and began to pray the sage. Pleased at this, Kapila offered to grant Anshuman a boon and the latter desired that his departed grand uncles' souls might get a place in heaven. Where upon the sage said: "That is possible only when the holy river Ganga comes down to the earth and washes their ashes with its holy waters. Then their souls might ascend to heaven."

Anshuman began the project of bringing down the Ganga from heavens which was subsequently taken by his son Dilip. Even Dilip couldn't complete the project and ultimately it was Dilip's son Bhagirath who completed the project of bringing down the holy river Ganga to earth. It is apparent that it was a long project and needed five generations' devoted toil to complete the mission. The holy river Ganga acquired yet another name Bhagirathi since it was Bhagirath who eventually brought it down really to the mortal plain.

[Hence the belief among the Hindus that washing the bones of their died relations with the Ganga water ensures their receiving a place in heavens.]

That of Soudasa

Bhagirath had the son named Suhotra and t ir dynasty continued this way; Suhotra> Shruti> Nabhag> Ambareesha> Sindhudweepa> Ayutayu> Rituparna> Sarvakaam> Suhas> Soudasa.

Soudasa was also called Mitrasaha. When he became the king, one-day he went out hunting in the forest and saw two tigers there. He killed one of these with his arrow and before dying, it adopted the form of a fierce Rakshasa (demon). The other tiger vowed: "I'll have my revenge and disappeared.

After some days King Soudasa began a Yagya. The Priest to conduct the ceremony was none other than sage Vashishta. After the ceremony was over. Vashishtha left but the rakshasa adopted Vashisitha form and sat down in Vashistha place. "At the end of the ceremony get me some rice and meat to eat." he ordered pompously," "I shall be returning in a short while." Having said this, the rakshasa went away. But nerreptitiously it adopted a cook's form and cooked some human meat. Unknowingly, King Soudasa placed this meat in a golden vessel and waited for Vashishtha's return.

When the same meat was served before Vashishtha, by his Yogic power, Vashishtha realised that this was human meat. So he cursed Soudasa for serving him human meat and said:" Be you a rakshasa (demon) this very moment." However Vashishtha by his divines power could also learn that this was not Soudasa's doing but of that rakshasa who adopted his own (Vashishtha's) form. So he modified his curse to Soudasa by saying that the duration of his curse would by only 12 years.

Nevertheless, Soudasa felt as if he was cursed for none of his fault. Enraged at sage Vashishtha imprudence, he at once took some water in his hand to curse Vashishtha in return. Seeing him ready, his wife Madayanti intervened:' "What racnilge are you committing? Don't curse the sage; he is our guru!"

Soudasa checked his anger. But what was to be done with the water he had taken in his hand to curse the sage? Since that water was charged with a mantra and was to be thrown by pronouncing the curse? Had it been thrown on the ground or up into the sky, it would have caused a big famine of water. Then there would have been no crop, no grain or food. So Soudasa thought be ter of throwing the water on to his own feet. With the result his feet became diseased and black. This earned him an epithet 'Kalmashapada' (one with defined or dirty feet).

Then passing the curse's snuthence for 12 years he lived as a rakshasa in the forest and ate people. In the forest he once happened to meet a brahmana and his wife. He proceeded to eat the brahmana neglecting the brahman's wife's request against it. This enraged the brahmana's wife as much as to curse him:" "You will die the moment you meet your wife."

Although after twelve years the king was freed of Vashistha's curse yet he refrained from going near his wife, fearing the curse from that brahmana's wife.

When Vashishtha learnt about the other curse, he realised that Soudasa's live would stop since he would not be able to copulate with his wife Madyanti. In order to provide a heir to the lineage Vashishta himself conceived Madayanti. But even for seven years she couldn't deliver. A last, grieved with the inborn son's refusal to come out she damaged her embryo with a stone. So the Child thus produced came to be named Ashmaka (making brought in the world by a stone). Then this dynasty continued his way: Ashmaka> Moolak> Deshratha> Ilivili> Vishwasaha> Khatvang> Deerghabahu> Raghu> Aja> Dashrath who had four renowned sons: Rama, Lakshmana, Bharata and Shatrughna. Rama's doings are very well recorded in various Ramayanas. He had defeated and killed Ravana. Bharata destroyed, three crores of Gandharvas. Shatrughana defeated a demon called Lavana and built the city of Mathura. Rama's son were Lava and Kusha; Lakashmana's Angada and Chandraketu; Bharata's Taksha and Pushkara and Shatrughna's; were Subahu and Sharasene. Vrihadala was the last ruler of this dynasty.

That of Nimi Ikshavaku's second sons name was Nimi. He once performed a Yagya lasting for a full 1000 years. Although Nimi wanted sage Vashishtha to be the chief priest of this Yagya, The sage expressed his inability saying that he was already busy in performing the Yagya arranged by the chief of gods, Indra, which was to last for about five hundred years. So he asked Nimi to wait and promised to join his ceremony as soon as his divine commitment was over.

Hearing this Nimi returned with the assumption that sage Vashishtha would come to his Yagya, on his part Vashishtha thought that Nimi would wait for his arrival. But Nimi requested sage Gautama who agreed to conduct the ceremony with the help of other sages Meanwhile, after conducting the Yagya Indra had arranged, Vashishtha came to Nimi's place with the expectation that Nimi would appoint him the chief priest. But, to his surprise, Vashishtha saw the Yagya already on with sage Gautama conducting the role of the chief priest. Vashishtha, owing to the confusion felt quite insulted. Getting angry Vashishtha cursed Nimi that he would henceforth be without a body. However, Nimi felt that the sage was unfair and cursing him for none of his fault. In retaliation he too cursed that Vashishtha would be without a body. But owing to his divine power Vashishtha managed to get a new body, thanks to his friendship to the gods Maitre and Varuna.

But, the sage Vashishtha's curse made Nimi lose his body. King Nimi's body lay there, at the site of the Yagya, oiled and perfumed. When the Yagya was over, the assembled gods wished to give the host of the Yagya a boon. They wished to give a new body to Nimi. But the king said he would have none of it. He desired instead that he might be allowed to live on the eyelids of the beings. The boon was eventually granted to him That is why King Nimi still lives and the eyelids of all beings. That is why the blinking of the eyes is known as 'mimesha' which literally means time taken to blink eyes once.

Nevertheless, another problem arose. Since king Nimi had no son, in the absence of a ruler his kingdom was sure to go to ruins. The sages and gods, then, deeided to produce a being from king Nimi's dead body. They began to pound it with wood and their continuos efforts eventually bore fruit. A son emerged from that body. Since the son came out in this fashion from his father's body, he came to be known as Janaka which literally means father (or creator). Moreover since he was produced by a father having no body he acquired yet another epithet: Vidiha which means without a body. When Janak was ploughing the earth to obtain a son, a daughter, came out of the earth. She is a renowned person, named Sita who was destined to become Lord Ram's spouse.

That of Chandra (Lunar Dynasty)

Having heard about the kings of the famous Solar Dynasty (of Ikshavaku and others) Maitreya then requested the sage, Parashar, to enlighten about the Chandra Vansha or Lunar Dynasty. This is what Parashar then told him.

Brahma had a son called Atri and Atri's Son was Chandra. It was Brahma who made Chandra (the Moon) the ruler of all stars, constillations and herbs. Getting this power Chandra also perfomed the royal sacrifice called Rajasooya Yagya which further enhanced his power. With his power this may enhanced substantially, Chandra grew somewhat arrogant. In his arrogance he dared to kidnap the wife of the divine Guru Brihaspati, called Tara. Despite Brahaspati's repeated request Chandra refused to return Tara. This made Brishaspati enraged and fierce war ensued between him and Chandra. Shukra, the priest and guru of demons, even otherwise, was not enamoured of the divine Guru Brihaspati. So he also sided with Chandra. Many demons influenced by Shukra also came to the side of Chandra. But Rudra and Indra continued to support Brihaspati.

Since Tara was the basic reason for this war, the whole war came to be known as Taramaya war. The war soon assumed such deadly proportions that it. appeared as if the whole world might be destroyed. This led every body to request Brahma to mediate to stop this war. Brahma took the role of the mediator and in no time the war was stopped and Tara was restored to Brihaspati.

Meanwhile, Chandra had produced a son-from Tara who was named Buddha. Buddha subsequently married Ila and their son was Puroorva. It was sometime back that Maitre and Varuna had cursed the divine danseuse Urvasi for some reason. They had cursed her that she would have to spend some time on the earth.

Once while Puroorva was roaming on the mount Gandhamadan, he happened to Spot Urvashi also enjoying the prestine moonlight. He fell for her and requested her to marry him. Urvasi accepted the proposal subject to a condition. It was that two sheep were to always stay close to her bed and if the sheep happened to be stolen by any one by any chance, she would immediately return to heaven. Since Puroorva was madly in love with Urvashi, he readily agreed to the condition. Then, he took Urvashi to his capital and they lived happily for as many as sixty thousand years.

Urvashi was also quite happy there and she had no desire to return to heaven. But in Urvashi's absence the Gandharvas felt very lonely in heaven. So they plotted ways of bringing back Urvashi to heaven. One night they managed to steal the two sheep. Since the accepted condition was broken, Urvashi immediately left back for heaven. However, during her stay with Puroorva she managed to beget six sons for Puroorva. The eldest among them was Ayu.

In fact Urvasi had three conditions put forth before Puroorva. Apart from the one relating to the sheep, the other conditions were that Urvashi should never see the king naked and that pure ghee was to be served to her for food. The Gandharvas knew the conditions. So first they stole the sheep. When in their separation Urvashi began to cry and challenge to Puroorva's masculinity, Puroorva ran after the Gandharvas in the dark unclad. But the Gandharavas also knew how to create fire in a typical way. When they created fire, in its glow Puroorva was also seen naked by Urvasi. Also, during this tussel. Urvasi was also not given the ghee diet. Since all the three conditions were broken, Urvasi left back for heaven. However, she assured Purvoorva that she will come back to deliver him their first son as she was now pregnant. This is how Ayu was born. Urvashi had also produced five other sons for Purvoorva. Their names were Amavasu, Vishwavasu, Shritrayu, Shataryu and Ayutaryu. In Amavashu's lineage was the sage Jahnu who had drunk the entire Ganga when the river descended on the earth and flooded his Ashrama. Then after the request of Bhagirath he released the river through his thigh.

While stealing the two sheep when the Gandharvas, were chased by Puroorva the former had told him the secret of producing Agni (fire) in a special way. They also instructed the king to divide the fire so created into three parts. It was Puroorva who with their assistance created Agni in three ways: Grihapatya, Ahavaniya and Dakshina. The three Agnis had their seperate significance. While the first one was for domestic usage, the second for inviting or invoking a great deity (or great soul) and the third was for fighting against the evil.

Puroorva lineage continued this way: Puroorva> Amavasu> Bhim> Kanchana> Suhotra> Jahnu> Sumathu> Ajapa> Valapashva> Kusha. Kusha had four sons called Kushamb, Kushanabh Adhoortaraja and Vasu. Kushamb had performed a great sacrifice to get a son as powerful as Indra. Frightened by that massive Yagya, Indra himself took birth as Kushamb's son. That son was called Gadhi. Gadhi had a beautiful daughter called Satyavati. She was married to the sage Richeeka against the gift of 1000 horses with black ears.

Satyawati And Richika

There is an interesting tale about Satyawati's marriage to the sage Richeeka. Though the sage wanted to marry Satyawati but her father had no desire to marry his daughter off to an old Brahamana having very hot-temper. So Gadhi demanded one thousand horses in return for his daughter. These horse, he demanded, were to be fast moving and white in colour but whose ears should be black. This was of course a difficult demand but the sage, Richeeka, managed to get such horses with the help of Varuna. Consequently his marriage to Satyavati was solemnized.

Now, Satyawati wanted a son. In order to fulfill his wife's this demand, Richeeka performed a Yagya and obtained some nice pudding as a result of that endeavour. But Satyawati put forth-another condition. She wished that her mother might also have a son. Richeeka, therefore prepared a second bowl of pudding. He gave the two bowls to Satyawati and said : "One is for you and other is for your mother". He then went off to forest to meditate.

But Satyawati's mother said:" People usually want godsons for themselves. They are not so keen about having a good brother-in-law. Hence my obvious suspicions is that your share of the nice pudding will be better than mine. But I request you to exchange the bowls. I am a queen and my son will surely be a ruler. While yours will be a brahmana. Since my son has to be stronger than yours, give me your share of the rice pudding." Satyawati was simpleton enough to accept the request and consequently the bowls were exchanged.

When Richeeka, the sage returned from the jungle and heard all that had transpired, he was very angry. It was because he had put the ingredients for a son who would be brave and violent as a Kshatriya into Satyawati's mother's bowl and in Satyawati's bowl he had mixed the ingredients to ensure a peaceful and non-violent son as a brahmana should be. But now, the consequences were reversed. When Satyawati learnt about it she was quite apologetic and begged for the mistake committed unknowingly" She requested that her grandson rather than her son should be brave and violent. At last Sage Richeeka granted the request. Consequently Satyawati's mother gave birth to Vishwamitra. And Satyawati gave birth to Jamdagni. Jamdagni, later on married Renuka. Their son was redoubtable Parashuram who killed many Kshatriya as he was quite violent and brave.

Vishwamitra had a son in due time called Sunahashesha who was later on, renowned as Devarat. Among the other sons of Vishwamitra were Madhuchhanda, Dhananjay, Kritadeya, Ashtak etc. which brought renown to the dynasty of Kaushika.

While telling about Ayu's dynasty sage Parashar said that Ayu was married to Rahu's daughter. Among his other sons were Nahusha, Kshatravriddha, Rambha, Raja and Aneha. The lineage continued from Kshatravriddha's son Suhota who has three sons: Kashya, Kaasha, and Gnittarsamada. Sage Shaunaka was the son of Gnittarsamada who had made the four division of society. Kashya's son was Kaushaya. Dhanvantari was the scion of this dynasty who is belived to be the author of Ayurveda, the most renowned indigenous school of medicine in India.

Raji's Tale

Puroorva's son Ayu had five sons. Their names were Nahusha, Kshatravriddha, Rambha Raji and Aneha. Now, Raji had five hundred brave sons. Many years ago, there ensued a fierce fight between the demons and the gods. Both the parties, being curious to know about the bad result of this fierce war, went to Brahma to know about it. They asked: "O Creator! Who will win this war?" Brahma replied that side would win the war which had Raji, the king fighting in its support.

Getting this hint the demons rushed to Raji and asked him to fight on their side. "I will", Raji said pompously,."Provided you promise to make me Indra after the devas (gods) have been defeated."

'Sorry, this we can't promise', replied the demons (Asuras) "We can't promise you something which we can't fulfil. Prahlad shall continue to be our Indra (ruler)'.

Then the gods also approached Raji and asked him to fight on their side. When King Raji repeated his condition, they replied, "Yes, indeed! You shall be our Indra."

Consequently, Raji joined the war from the gods' side and managed to defeat the demon. After the enemy had been defeated, Indra touched Raji's feet and said: "Since you have protected us, you are like our father. And since I am Indra, my father is obviously the supreme ruler of the world". Although Raji saw through this flattery the cunningness of the chief of gods, he permitted Indra to continue as the king of the gods and returned to his capital.

However, following Raji's death, Raji's son demanded that Indra should hand over that which had been promised to them. But Indra refused to comply with this request. This made Raji's son-furious and they defeated Indra and assumed the title of the Indra themselves. They remained on the heaven's throne for many years. Then Indra, at last went to Vrihaspati and prayed that his kingdom might be returned to him. The divine Guru then performed many special sacrifice in order to endow Indra with the powers, he had lost. Slowly he also made certain arrangement to see that Raji's arrogant sons were weaned away from the righteous path. This made them do many evil deeds and turn their minds away from the holy Vedas and however to brahmana. Indra now could again defeat them and kill the sons of Raji to get back his divine kingdom.

Nahusha And Yayati

Ayu's first son was Nahusha. Nahusha had six sons. Their name was Yati, Yayati, Samyati, Ayati, Viyati and Kriti. Among these Yati was a man of ascetic like temperament. He had no desire to be a king. With the result, Yayati became the king after Nahusha. Yayati had two wives. The first was Shukracharya's daughter Devyani and the second was the demon-lord Vrishaparva's daughter Sharmishtha. He got two sons from Devyani who were called Yadu and Turvasu, and two from Sharmistha were Druhya Anu and Puru.

Owing to a curse Yayati had received from Shukra he had become much old before he should have been. Then he called his son Yadu and said: "Son! I have become old rather untimely. But I still want to enjoy material and sensual pleasures. Would you lend me your youth and accept my old age for 1000 years." Yadu refused to comply with the request which made his father curse him: "I say in your line no son would be worthy of being a king. Your (Yadu's) dynasty would be devoid of any worthy king. Then he summoned Turvasu, Druhya and Anu. But they also refused to part with their youth against the exchange of their father's old age. Consequently Yayati also imposed upon them the same curse which he had on Yadu. Finally he summoned Puru who immediately agreed to his father's request. He took upon himself his father's old age and gave in return his own youth.

Becoming young Yayati immersed himself in all sensual pleasures. But after having spent many years in sensual pursuits he developed surfeit with them. Then he got back his old age from Puru and returned Puru's youth back to him. Yayati made Puru the king and went off to do penance in the forest. Since Turvasu, Druhya and Anu and stubbornly refused to agree to their father's request they only received small kingdom eventually from their unhappy father.

It was in Yadu's line that Arjuna was born. He received several boons from Dattatreya following his devoted service to the learned sage. One of them was that Arjuna be endowed with a 1000 arms. The second was Arjuna's commitment to wage a constant fight against unrighteous conduct to establish proper Dharma. He was also committed to fighting the evil and serve the good. The third boon was no enemy would be able to defeat him (Arjuna). And finally the fourth was that Arjuna could be killed only by someone renowned in the three worlds. This Arjuna came to be renowned as Kartaveeryaarjuna. With these powers he performed as many as ten thousands Yagyas and could rule for 85 thousand years. His capital was Mahishmati Nagari. Once Ravana of the Ramayana fame dared to invade his capital and was defeated and imprisoned by Arjuna. This brave Arjuna was eventually killed by Parashuram, the scourge of the Kshatriya class. All those who descended from Yadu came to be known as Yadavas the most prominent among Them was Lord Krishna of the Gita fame. He was once involved in a false charge of stealing the priceless gem, called Syamantak Mani. The story is given ahead.

The Tales from Dwapar and Kali Ages

The Tale Related to the Famous Gem Syamantak

Krishna was born in Yadu's Vansha (dynasty). He was the most renowned figure of the Dwaper Age. One of his wives was Satyabhama whose brother was Satyajit. He was a staunch devotee of the sun god. One day he sat down on the shores of the ocean and began to pray Surya (the son god). The deity was propitiated by Satyajit rigorous phance and appeared before him, dazzling the devotee's eyes with his unmatched brilliance. With the result, Satyajit couldn't see Surya and requested:"Lord I can't see you clearly in your dazzling brilliance. Even in the sky you appear like a burning ball of fire. I request you to make me see you clearly."

At this request Surya put off the brilliant Jewel known as Syamantaka Mani tied around his throat. Now Satyajit could see the deity clearly. Surya's eyes were brownish yellow and his body hue was bright like a radiating copper Satyajit them bowed his head down before Surya and Surya offered to grant him any boon. Satyajit then requested to have the jewel and Surya readily granted it to him.

Putting it round his neck Satyajit entered the city of Dwarika. But because of the jewel he was wearing his body appeared radiant with energy seemed to be flowing out of him. Looking at him the citizens of Dwarika felt as though the deity Sun had come in their midst.

Reaching his house Satyajit kept the jewel secretly hidden. The gem had the divine power of producing gold in a fixed quantity everyday.

And due to its divine influence all disease, drought, wild animals, fire and events of theft vanished from the region. Krishna, learning about the divine powers of the gem thought that such a precious jewel must remain in the custody of the king of the region, Ugrasen. Satyajit knew about Krishna's this desire. Scared that he might be compelled to part with the jewel, he gave it to his brother Prasen for safe keeping. However the quality of the gem was that it would yield the fixed amount of gold everyday only when someone pure of heart and intentions held it. It could even kill the holder if he had an impious heart.

One day Prasen went for hunting wearing the jewel on his neck. As his bad luck would have it, in the jungle he was killed by a lion. It was when the lion was about to eat its prey that Jamvant, the king of bears of Ramayan fame, happened to reach there. Seeing the lion about to eat up dead man, Jamvant killed the lion. He returned home taking the jewel along. He gave the jewel to his young son to play with.

Meanwhile, the citizens of Dwarika noticed Prasen's absence from the city for long. Upon enquiry they learnt about his having gone for hunting a couple of days before. Since most of them were aware about Krishna's supposed craving for the divine jewel they spread the rumour that Krishna has secretly usurped the jewel after having killed Prasen in the jungle. The citizens knew that Krishna wanted that jewel so the rumour had gained momentum. Krishna was disturbed for being falsely accused of the theft. In order to put an end to such rumour, he decided to follow the path Prasen might have taken. The trail led him to the forest. There he discovered two dead bodies: one of a lion and one of Prasen. He guessed what might have happened. So he went on searching for a clue and reached Jamvant's cave. There he found a young bear playing with the gem. Seeing him approaching the nursemaid of the Child raised an alarm that brought Jamvant also there. Then a fierce fight ensued between the two. This fight went on for 21 days. When Krishna didn't return several Yadava soldiers also went in his search and eventually reached near Jamvant's hole. When nearly a week passed and still they couldn't find any trace of Krishna they concluded that Krishna might have also been killed. So they returned spreading the news about Krishna's supposed death.

Having learnt about this sorry news, Krishna's friends and relation arranged for the Shraddha ceremony of the supposedly departed soul. This ceremony provided a kind of astral strength to Krishna still fighting with Jamvant. This additional strength made Krishna defeat Jambavant. Then the two became friends and the bear-lord married off his daughter Jambavati to Krishna who returned home with a new bride and the precious gem recovered.

The citizens of Dwarika were delighted to find Krishna back and coming back with his bride Jambavati. Krishna then told them all that had transpired and returned the jewel to Satyajit. Satyajit was quite ashamed that he had ever doubted Krishna's integrity. In repentence he apologised to Krishna and also married his sister Satyabhama to him.

However, Satyabhama's marriage to Krishna created trouble among the Yadava clan. Owing to Satyabhama's beauty, Akroora, Kritaverma and Shatadhanwa also wanted to marry her. They felt slighted and started weaving a plot against Satyajit. It was around this time that Krishna learnt that the Pandavas had barely escaped getting burnt in Varanavrat. So immediately he left to meet his Cousins[1] and learn about their welfare. Taking the advantage of Krishna's absence Shatadhanwa managed to killed Satyajit. Satyabhama was furious and she immediately left in a Chariot to apprise Krishna of these sorry tidings. Shatadhanwa had not only killed Satyajit but he also managed to steel the Symantaka Mani.

Learning about these turn out of the events Krishna returned to Dwarika with Satyabhama.Krishna then told his elder brother Baladeva about Shatadhanwa's heinous deed. Then both the brothers decided to punish Shatadhanwa by death. Although Shatadhanwa had fled to Akroora and Kritavarma's palaces for safety, the twosome failed to rescue their friend from the wrath of Krishna and Baladeva. However, before fleeing away Shatdhanwa had managed to pass on the precious gem to Akroora's custody. Nobody knew that the gem was now in Akroora's custody.

Meanwhile, chasing Shatadhanwa, both Krishna and Baladeva reach as far out as in Mithila Kingdom. Shatadhanwa was on the horse but

---

[1]The Pandava's mother Kunti was sister of Krishna's father.

the animal died after such a long journey. Then Krishna chased him on foot, asking Baldeva to wait for him in the Chariot. Eventually, Krishna managed to catch Shatadhanwa and beheaded him with his mighty weapon, the renowned Chakra Sudarshan. But Krishna despite his searching the whole body of and clothes of Shatadhanwa, failed to recover the gem. He came back to the chariot and reported the matter to Baldeva, Baldeva, however, did not believe his brother's word. He said: "Krishna, I knew you had an eye on the gem. You have a thieving disposition right since childhood and hence I don't believe you. In fact you are not the brother I would like to associate with. Now you go your own way and I will go mine. Henceforth we are not united." With these angry words Baldeva went off to the kingdom of Videha and lived there as a guest of king Janaka. It was when he was returning that he met Duryodhan on way. On the Kaurava prince's request he decided to pass some days in Hastinapur. There he taught Duryodhan the nuances of wielding the mace (gada). Meanwhile, Krishna was in Dwarika. He was still sad over the death of Satyajit and the loss of the Syamanteka Mani. After three years had passed, Vabhnu, Ugrasena and other Yadavas, managed to convince Baldeva that Krishna had, indeed, not stolen the jewel. It was after much cajoling and coaxing that Baldeva agreed to return to Dwarika and patch up with his brother, Krishna.

All this while Akroora was having a swell time. Since he had the jewel he was growing rich. So he started performing many sacrifices. Owing to his possessing that divine gem the things were very auspicious in Dwarika. This gave all the impression as if peace and plenty in Dwarika was reigning owing to Akroora's doing so many religious sacrifices. But when Akroora went outside Dwarika for some days, Dwarika again started having all kinds of famines and diseases plaguing the city. Again, this led people to believe that a noble person like Akroora's going out of the region was causing all this trouble. However, seeing their developments Krishna grew suspicious. He knew that all these drastic changes in the general well being of the people of Dwarika could have been caused by the presence of the divine gem. And the people of Dwarika were feeling troubled only because the gem was no more there. So, he deduced, also by seeing sudden prosperity in

Akroora's house that the divine gem must be in Akroora possession.

Meanwhile returning home Akroora again started to perform many Yajanas. He thought: "Even if Krishna has suspicion about my possessing the previous gem be won't come to kill me since I am performing the Yagyas and it is a heinous crime to kill anyone performing the holy Yagyas." So, the sacrifices went on for as many as sixty-two years. And because the Jewel was in Dwarika, disease and other evil things disappeared from the city. This further confirmed all the suspicions that Krishna had about Akroora possessing the gem.

So, One day he called an assembly of the Yadava clan and disclosed his suspicion in the presence of Akroora. "We all know that Shatadhanwa had left the Syamantak Mani with you. Let the jewel remain with you. There is no harm in that. In fact we all are gaining from its presence in Dwarika. But Baldeva suspects I have stolen it. Will you please show it to him once to dispel the suspicion about my stealing it?"

Akroora, for a moment, was in a fix. Then he reasoned that if he lied they might search his clothes and discover the jewel. So he took out the jewel himself from a golden box that he kept hidden inside his clothes. He offered it to the Yadava who was to be considered by the assembly most worthy of possessing it.

The jewel was really so captivating that all began to cover it including Baldeva and Satyabhama. Satyabhama thought "I have an additional right over it since it was won by my brother from Suryadeva." Studying their greedy reactions, Krishna felt that a bloody quarrel was imminent. So, he intervened." Well, you all know that only a man of noble intentions and conduct should possess it. If someone of impure heart happens, to wear it, the wearer is sure to be destroyed. But who is that Kind of noble man or women in our midst? I am not the deserving one because I have more than 16000 woman. For the same reason, let not Satyabhama possess it. After all, it is to be earned by merit and it can't be bequeathed to anyone. Nor should Baldeva deserve it as he keeps on having all kind of narcotic drinks. So, in my opinion, let it stay with Akroora. At least he is using the wealth he is getting from the gem in conducting noble sacrifices." This was agreeable to all and this was how Krishna kept his clam united.

Shishupal Story: Shishupal was the son of the fifth daughter of Shoorswa who was married to Chidi King Damagosha Shishupal was also Krishna's close relation, being the son of the sister of Krishna's father Vasudeva. He had also some additional body parts when he was born. It was claimed that his potential slayer would have his additional body part falling down automatically the moment the infant went on to that person's lap. It was eventually proved to be Krishna himself because when Krishna took the infant Shishupal in his lap, Shishupal's additional body-part fell off. Seeing this, Shishupal's mother Shrutashrava was frightened. Then she asked Krishna to be considerate to her son. Krishna had promised that he would pardon Shishupal's 100 offences but in the event of his committing 101st offence, he would behead Shishupal as ordained by the Providence. This Krishna did during the Rajsooya Yagya performed by the Pandavas in which Shishupal kept on abusing Krishna. Krishna bore with patience his abusing and the moment he abused Krishna for 101st time he beheaded the offender with his Sudarshan Chakra in the open assembly of the Rajsooya Yagya. It is said that in an earlier life Shishupal had been Hiranyakashyapu — the demon lord who was slayed by Vishnu in his Narisimha incarnation. Just as Hiranyakashyapu was slain by Vishnu, Shishupal was slain by Krishna in this life. The Purana also claims that Shishupal had also been born as Ravana in his one of the previous life when he was slain by Vishnu in the incarnation as Rama.

The Tales of Kuru's Dynasty, Shantanu and Devapi

Continuing the narration of the dynasty of Kuru, sage Parashar told Maitreya that in the line of Kunu there used to be a king called Pratipa. Pratipa had three sons: Devapi, Shantanu and Vahleeka. Since Devapi had renounced the world to perform penance at a very young age, Shantanu became the king.

Some years after Shantanu's becoming the king, it so happened that for 12 years in a row there was no rain in his kingdom. Then Shantanu invited all the rishis and learned brahmanas to know the reason behind famine gripping his kingdom. The learned assembly informed him that since rightfully Devapi should have been the king, the nature was showing its wrath. The eldest son's this claim could be rejected in preference of the younger ones only when the eldest son be and outright sinner or physically incapable to rule. Hence in order to propitiate nature, it was essential that Devapi was called back from the forest and installed at the royal throne.

Shantanu had an able minister named Ashmasuri. This minister arranged a preacher to go to Devapi in the forest. However, reaching there the preacher preached against the Vedas. Gradually the preacher brainwashed Devapi in such a way as to turn the latter 's mind away from the Holy Scriptures. But when led by the holy Brahmanas Shantanu went to Devapi to offer the kingdom to the latter, to their amazement they found Devapi mouthing foul words against the holy Vedas. This way Dewapi had become a sinner and hence undeserving to get the throne. Eventually Shantanu continued to rule and nature also accepted him as the king. Consequently, it rained normally and all was well in Hastinapur.

Continuing to give details of this dynasty, sage Parashar said that Shantanu had two wives. One of them was Ganga (the river) who gave Shantanu a redoubtable son called Devvrat popularly called Bhishma for his taking a terrible vow upon himself for the entire life of perpetual celibacy and bachelor-hood. Shantanu's other wife was Satyavati and she bore him two sons: Vichitraveerya and Chitrangada. Dhritarashtra and Pandu were descended from 'Vichitraveerya. Dhritarashtra had 100 sons from his wife named Gandhari while Pandu had five sons from his two wives Kunti and Madri. The Pandavas common wife was Draupadi and she bore five sons for each of them. Her sons' names were Prativindhya, Sutasoma, Shrutakriti, Shatanika and Shrutakarma. Apart from these five the Pandavas (sons of Pandu) also had other sons from their other wives. Yudhisthir married Yudheja and had a son called Devaka. Bhim married Hidamba and their son's name was Ghatotkachha. Bhim had yet another wife named Kashi who bore him a son called Sarvatraga. Arjuna the famous archer had many wives. From Subhadra he had a son named Abhimanyu, from Chitrangada, Babruvahana and from Ulupi, Iravan.

Vasudeva And Devaki

Vasudeva, the son of Shoorsena married Devaka's daughter Devaki. Devaki's cousin Kansa was the son of Ugrasena, the ruler of Mathura. At the time of Devaki's marriage Kansa drove the chariot of the newly married couple. At this time a divine voice had thundered from the sky saying: "Stupid Kansa! Do you know whose chariot are you driving? The eighth child of this very couple will kill you!"

Hearing the warning Kansa thought the best way to get rid of the threat was to kill this woman Devaki immediately. So he took up his sword and wanted to kill Devaki. But Vasudeva checked him with the request: "O brave warrior! Don't kill your sister rest assured that I will hand over to you every children she produces". Kansa agreed to this arrangement.

It was at that time that Prithvi (earth) was also feeling badly suppressed by the weight of the sinners. So taking the form of a cow she went to the gods on the mount Sumeru and made her complaint. She narrated her tale of woes, saying that evil doers had come on the earth and they were creating havoc.

They were distressing all the noble persons. Many years ago demon called Kalinemi had been destroyed by Vishnu. This Kalinemi had taken the birth in the form of Kansa now. He has made all the vile persons now acting as the evil but powerful kings like Arishtha, Dhenuka, Keshi, Pralamba, Naraka, Sunda and Vanasur come together. Together they had emerged as a dominant evil force and now severely distressing the earth.

Brahma endorsed all that the earth had said and suggested "Let's go to the northern shores of the great ocean to pray Vishnu for providing relief to you. Vishnu always incarnates every time you suffer this kind of trouble. It is about time he incarnated to help the revival of the Dharma and extermination of Adharma."

When the earth in the cow's form, led by Brahma and other gods reached the great ocean to say their prayers, Vishnu appeared before them. He said while to tearing off two shreds of hair from his breed: "Then two hairs of mine will be born on the earth to destroy the Asuras". Then with a pause he said:" "All of these gods will also be born on earth to fight with the Asuras." Before disappearing he also added: "I shall come to the earth as the eight child of Devaki."

Meanwhile Narad Conveyed all these divine tiding to Kansa who blew up hearing the divine conspiracy. Immediately he imprisoned both Devaki and Vasudeva with the instructions to the guards to tell him about the birth of any child to this couple. One by one six sons were born to Devaki and Kansa killed each of them.

Vasudeva had another wife known as Rohini who lived in Gokul. When Devaki was pregnant for the seventh time the embryo was magically transferred to Rohini's womb by a divine scheme. With the result Kansa never got a chance to slay the seventh son who later came to be known as Baladeva, also called Samkarshana because he happened to change the course of the river Yamuna.

When Devaki became pregnant for the eighte times, owing to Lord Vishnu's entry into her womb she looked so bright that no one could bear a glare at her. Vishnu as Krishna was finally born in the lunar month of Bhadrapada on the 8th day at the middle of the night. Getting the hint all the sages rejoiced at Vishnu's this incarnation. The Gandharvas sang and the Apsaras danced. The gods showered flowers at the prison where Krishna was born.

However, the danger of Kansa killing this child also very much loomed large. In order to escape the danger Vasudeva proposed to take the infant somewhere else. As the providence willed, the guards of the prison remained asleep and the gates of the prison also opened. The chains that were binding Vasudeva and Devaki also fell away by Vishnu's grace.

It was raining very heavily that night. As Vasudeva put the infant in a wicker basket to take it across Yamuna on foot, the river became very much swollen. Perhaps it wanted to touch the feet of the infant. Then, the moment it touched the infant feet it subsided. Although it was still raining but the great serpent, Shesh Nag, came up spreading its 1,000 hoods to protect the child. Weathering these troubles Vasudeva eventually managed to bring the infant on the other bank of Yamuna and deposited at the bed of Yashoda, the wife of his friend Nanda, who had delivered a daughter at that very time. This way Vasudeva exchanged the infants and taking along the newly born daughter of Nanda reached back to his prison. Then magically everything became as normal as before the birth of the child. Then the daughter of Nanda, called Yogamaya started crying. Hearing the cry the guards of the prison woke up and they dutifully informed their master, Kansa, about the birth of yet another child in the prison.

Hearing the news, Kansa rushed to the prison, picked up the baby and threw it down at the stone to kill it. But Yogmaya was really a goddess who had been sent by Vishnu. When Kansa tried to throw it down, the baby rose up into the air and adopted the eight-arm form of the goddess. "Stupid Kansa", she said, "the person destined to slay you has already taken birth. It was he who had also killed you in your last birth." So declaring and leaving Kansa rather bewildered Yogmaya vanished into the sky.

Now Kansa called all his evil friends together to say: "My friends! The mischievous gods have again conspired to kill me and weaken us because we are brave. But I am least daunted by their conspiracy. You know well my powers that had once forced even Indra to flee like a coward before my keen arrows. Barring my guru Jarasandha I am not sacred of any one. These pranks of the gods make me laugh with derision. Nevertheless, one has to be careful seeing one's enemies active. I have learnt that Devaki's this escaped eighth child will kill me. So we must eliminate any such child which bears any resemblance with that child of Devaki. Look for any strong infant and slay it immediately.

Then he released Vasudeva and Devaki while feigning his repentence for killing their children. "I didn't kill your children unnecessarily. This was their fate. The person destined to kill me has now taken birth some where else."

Krishna's Valour In Childhood
1. Slaying of Pootana and other Incidents
On Kansa's advice his all friends and well-wishers had spread in the entire region to search for a male child with unusual strength.

Meanwhile, as was customary Nanda and other cowherd chiefs had come to Mathura to pay taxes to the king. Nanda also went to meet his recently released friend Vasudeva who congratulated the latter for getting a son. Although Vasudeva Knew yet he didn't tell Nanda that his son was really the son of the former. Nevertheless, he told Nanda to quickly return to Gokula and look after his son as well as Vasudeva's other son (Baladeva) who was also staying with Nanda. The cowherds were also eager to return to Gokula as they had heard about the royal order for killing the robust younglings of the region.

On the night they returned from Gokula they asked their wives to be wary about any unfamiliar knower.

One night in Gokula, Putana, a demoness and confident of Kansa, came to feed the young Krishna, in a comely form as she had heard about this most captivating child of the region. Putana had poison in her breast and any child fed by her was sure to die. She started breast-feeding Krishna with the same intention. But Krishna grasped Putana firmly and began to drink life out of her. Soon Putana collapsed and died. On yet another occasion, the baby Krishna was lying down under a cart. He felt hungry and so he was crying and kicking his legs up in the air. As a result of his kicking the cart got overturned and all the pots and vats that were on the cart got broken. Everyone came running to see what had happened. They were surprised to find that such a small baby had overturned a huge cart. In fact that cart was the changed form of a demon called Shakatasur who was detected and killed by infant Krishna. Yashoda lovingly embraced her child and worshipped the gods for saving her son's life.

When Krishna and Baldeva became relatively safe, the sage Ganga was invited to Gokula by Nanda. Sage Ganga named Rohini's son as Rama (or Balarama) and Yashoda's as Krishna. Soon the babies learnt to crawl and smeared with cowdung they roamed around their home merrily. They were two captivating to behold and hence became the centre of attraction. At times the two infant brothers would crawl into the cowsheds and playfully pulled the tails of the calves. One day Yashoda, irritated by her infant son Krishna's pranks, tied him to a thresher. Then she remained busy in her domestic chores. Krishna, meanwhile, pulled and tugged at the thresher. There were two huge trees closeby that were quite close to each other. Krishna went about crawling and dragged the thresher in these two trees while trying to pass through the space through them. But the thresher got stuck in the space between the two trees. As child Krishna pulled and tugged the huge trees were uprooted and fell down to the ground. The loud thud of the falling trees brought everyone there. They were amazed as to how the two sturdy trees were felled by a mere child's tugging the thresher. Child Krishna, undaunted by the disturbance, sat there amongst the wreckage smiling gleefully. The rope that Yashoda had tied around his waist was still there. The tying of the rope around his waist earned another epithet for Krishna: DAMODAR which literally means he who has a 'Dama (rope) around his Udar (stomach).

However, despite Krishna escaping these hurdles unscathed, the people of the region reckoned the hurdles as being bad omens. They worshipped many deities to keep safe their beloved 'Kanha' — as they lovingly addressed Child Krishna. Little were they aware that the one who was born to end the entire creations miseries was unassailable by any mortal trouble. Nevertheless fearing other troubles lying in store for their beloved Kanha they decided to leave Gokula for Vrindavan, bag and baggage.

Balrama and Krishna grew up there. They looked after the cows, played in the open fields near the holy river Yamuna; they wore peacock feathers on their heads. Krishna particularly became a deft flute player. The sound of his flute was so captivating that it would force the cowmaidens called Gopis to assessable round him and dance to his flute tune. Prominent among them was two Gopis Shakha and Vishakha.

Kaliya Humbled

Part of Yamuna close to the bank was polluted by a huge snake called Kaliya. He lived there with his family. Because the snake lived there all the trees along the banks were scorched owing to snake puking toxic vapours. The snake was quite a huge being and equally dreadful. The people shunned that bank of Yamuna because of the snake Kaliya's presence. And if any birds flew over the area, the water made toxic by snake's exhalations struck them down. Krishna realised that this snake was none other than the snake which had once been defeated by his mount Garuda as Vishnu, in the ocean. Having fled the ocean the snake had made its home that pit of Yamuna popularly called Kali-Daha. Since that snake's presence was making the bank of the river hazardous for all, Krishna decided to kill that snake.

Once while he was playing with a ball with his friends, he deliberately made the ball into that part of the river. Since the ball belonged to his friend, his that friend threatened Krishna to retrieve it. Krishna, tying his clothes firmly around the body jumped into the river from a nearly Kadamba tree. His splash in the water made bits of water strike the trees close by which started to burn because of the toxic effect of the water of the river.

Krishna, meanwhile, merrily dived into the river's depth and then began to swim at the bottom to retrieve the ball. On hearing the sound, Kailya quickly arrived there. His eyes were red with anger and flames issued out of his mouth. He was surrounded on all sides by smaller snakes and female snakes of his family. While the snakes began to close in on Krishna, Krishna started dancing with such alacrity that the snakes got no chance to bite him.

Meanwhile when his friends didn't find Krishna returning to the shore early, they felt nervous and reported the matter to the elders. Hearing the disturbing news about Krishna jumping into the poisonous waters, all including Nanda, Yashoda and Balarama rushed to the bank of the river. "Where is my beloved Kanha?" screamed Yashoda in utter nervousness. They did get a glance of Krishna dancing amidst the snakes. This view made the women of Vrindavan cry and men nervous. But Balarama pacified them and signalled Krishna to end the Kaliya menace.

Krishna at once shook off the cooling snakes and jumped on their leader Kaliya's hoods. There he began to dance frenzically, causing pain to the snake whose hoods began to bleed. Whenever the snake tried to raise his hood, Krishna stamped it down with his feet. At last the snake began to vomit blood and became unconscious. Seeing their lord's pitiable conditions all the she snakes began to pray Krishna, begging for mercy. They requested to spare Kaliya's life. Kaliya also regained consciousness and he also joined his wives to request Krishna to spare their lives. Krishna agreed to let them go on the condition that they all would go back to the ocean and would never return to any river. It is claimed that till now snakes have Krishna's feet stamped on their hoods. It is only after seeing this stamp that Garuda would not pester them.

At last Krishna triumphantly emerged from Yamuna, having humbled Kaliya and thus ensuring purity of the river's water.

Dhenukasur Slayed

Near Vrindavan there was a lovely orchard full of sweet and delicious fruits hanging from the trees. One day wandering around the forest Balarama and Krishna happened to reach near that orchard. Looking at the fruits hanging from the trees they wished to eat them. "But their friends advised them, "You should be doing it at a great risk. Their lives a demon in the form of a donkey who survived on deer meat. This orchard is also under his control."

Whereupon Balrama said: "Don't worry for that donkey and help yourselves with juicy and sweet fruits." But still scared, the boys requested Krishna and Balrama to pluck some fruits for them. They both jerked the trees so violently that many fruits fell on to the ground. But the commotion attracted the angry Dhenukasur, the donkey. With his bind legs the donkey kicked Balrama in the chest. But Balrama caught hold of those two legs and began to twirl the donkey round and round. Then he tossed it away, causing the donkey instant death. Hearing the noise many assistants of the demon also reached there but Krishna killed them single handedly. This made that lovely orchard safe and the cowboys began to enjoy its fruits while grazing their cattle.

Killing of the Demon Pralamble

Having killed the demon Dhenukasur, Krishna and Balaram reached beneath a huge banyan tree. There they indulged in a variety of games which including plucking the flowers and making the garlands. In their playful mirth they also made ropes to be tied round the shoulders of their cattle. While they were having their games, a demon named Pralamb happened to join their friends disguised as a cowherd boy (Gopa). Pralamb thought that Krishna might be too strong to kill so he targeted his evil designs at Balarama. At that time the boys were playing a special kind of game which involved a race to particular point. Then the loser was to carry the winner upon his shoulder. The first pair to compete in the game was Krishna and Sudama in which Krishna emerged as the victor. Next was the turn of Balarama and the other Gopa (Pralamb) Balarama easily defeated Pralamb. Now, as per the condition of the race, Pralamb was to carry Balaram upon his shoulder. This he did but instead of running in the decided direction Pralamb ran in the opposite one with Balarama upon his shoulder. It was only after a while that Balarama realised his mate's real intentions. While doing so Pralamb also adopted the size of a huge mountain and his eyes were as large as the cartwheels.

Balarama was panicky. He yelled: "Krishna! I am being kidnapped! What will I do?" "Why ask me", Krishna replied non-challengly."You are strong enough to kill this demon! Beat him to death!"

Balarama suddenly became charged with anger. His eyes became red with rage. He beat down on the head of the demon with his strong fists. The blows were too strong for the demon to bear and he eventually died, puking out bloods from his mouth.

Indra Humbled

It was customary in the Viraj region to worship the lord of rains, Indra at the end of the rainy season. When the rains were over the local population decided to observe a special Yagya to honour Indra. They believed that it was this lord that controls the rain-laden clouds. They knew that without rains there would have been no grains. So they celebrated this ritual worship of Indra as a thanks-giving ceremony.

However, Krishna was opposed to this worship of Indra. He was now a grown up lad and he told his foster father, Nanda: "Father! We are neither farmers nor traders. We dwell in the Vanas (jungles) and survive through animal husbandry. Hence our gods should be cattle and the mountains. It is, therefore, logical that instead of worshipping Indra we start worshipping our mountains which provide fodder and water to our cattles. In this respect our mount Goverdhan deserves a dedicated worhsip. We must worship it in place of Indra."

All the Gops (the cow-men) and their chief saw much sense in what Krishna said. So, instead of worshipping Indra they decided to hold especial ceremony to worship the mount Goverdhan. They offered various choicest eatables to their cattle and anointed the mouth with holy water, ghee and curds. Following this they threw a big feast in which brahmanas and guests were sumptuously fed.

Meanwhile, Indra, expecting a devoted worship was amazed that he was being neglected against a mere mount Goverdhan. He became very angry and decided to teach the people of the Vraj region a bitter lesson."How dare they neglect me, the chief of the gods, and master of rains," he thundered. Immediately he summoned the dark clouds laden with water and said: "Listen to what I say," he instructed them naughtily "Go and destroy the cattle with rain and wind. I will come on my mount Airavat (the elephant) to pour down thick stream of rain as well."

Soon it began to rain cats and dogs in Vraj region with wind intensifying the rains. There were dark and ferocious looking clouds everywhere. The rainwater began to inundate the living places of the peoples and cattles both. All were severely distressed with fierce, cyclonic rains Cows and cattles began to die.

Krishna realised the foul intentions of Indra. Now he had to do something to protect his people and cattles. He immediately went to the mount Goverdhan and uprooted it. Then he kept it balanced on his tiny finger, thus providing a huge umbrella of protection. He asked the people to come beneath this huge umbrella for protection from the blinding rains. They came under it and got relief from the ferocious rains which Indra kept showering down the region in his maddening fury, But no matter what he did he couldn't trouble either the people or the cattle of the region of Vraj. After that Indra gave up resigned, by and Krishna returned the mountain to the original spot.

Soon Indra came down to apologise before Krishna: "O Lord! In my silly fury I forgot that you are the Lord Supreme who has come down the earth to redeem it from the evil and establish the righteous rule. You saved all the cattles and people. Henceforth you shall be called Govinda, the master of the cows.

Then Indra took down a bell hanging around Atravat's neck, filled it with holy water and ceremonially anointed Krishna. Then Indra also requested Krishna to look after his psychic son Arjuna, the third Pandava. Then bowing reverentially Indra left back to his realm, singing Krishna as Vishnu's praises.

Other Feats Accomplished In Childhood

It was after the Goverdhan Pooja that the local cowherd could realise that their Kanha was not an ordinary person. Although this realisation made them a bit scared, Krishna readily assured them that he was their true friends and well wisher.

One day demons deft in disguising himself in various guises reached there in the form of a bull. His name was Arishta. The bull was as dark as the rain-laden clouds. The horns were sharp and pointed and his eyes were as bright as the sun. He tore up the ground with his hooves. He was so tall that it was impossible to climb over him. He as the bull became a scourge of the hapless cows and calves. The bull looked so ferocious that everybody was frightened at the demon Arishtha's arrival. But, undaunted, Krishna decided to take on him. He clapped his hands, challenging a duel. On hearing the sound of the clap, Arishtha charged at Krishna with horns lowered. But Krishna grasped the horns and stopped the bull. Then he hit Arishtha with his thighs. Finally he tore up one of the horns and attacked Arishtha with it, throwing it away. The demon puked blood and died instantly.

Meanwhile, Narada related all of Krishna's exploits to Kansa and he was enraged. Now he realised who could be his potential slayer. So he decided that Balarama and Krishna must be killed before they become more powerful and sturdy. He made arrangements to ensure their killing. He had two murderous wrestlers called Chanoor and Mushtik. He plotted to have Krishna and Balarma killed by them in a wrestling competition. He announced that a massive wrestling competition would be held and invited all the wrestlers for this. He sent his friend Akroora especially to bring Krishna and Balarama. He also asked his elephant-trainer to ready his deadly elephant called Kuvalyapada to crush the two brothers to death. Meanwhile, taking no chances he asked a demon called Kashi to go to Vrindavan and kill the two brothers before their advent in Mathura.

Kashi adopted the form of a horse and went to Vrindavan. He tore up the earth with his hooves became as big as to shake the clouds with his manes and attacked the sun and the moon on his way to Vrindavana. The cowherds were naturally frightened.

But Krishna faced Kashi regularly. He inserted his hands into the horse's mouth and broke off the horse's teeth. Like bits of white clouds one by one the teeth fell-down on the ground. Then Krishna tore off the demon's lips and Kashi began to vomit blood. His eyes also fell off. Krishna then tore Kashi into two parts with his bare hands. The killing of the demon Kashi earned Krishna yet another epithet: Keshava, meaning killer of Kashi.

Meanwhile, Akroora also arrived there and told Krishna and Balarama about the royal invitation. The two brothers sensed Kansa's intentions and accepted the invitations. Although the whole of Vrindavana and Gokula were against their going to Mathura, Krishna convinced them about the vital need of his going to Mathura. Then sitting in the Chariot with Akroora both Krishna and Balaram set out for Mathura.

Kansa Trounced And killed

Both the brothers reached Mathura with Akroora in the evening. While Akroora went straight to the palace, both the brothers got down in the city with the promise of reaching the Venue of the wrestling competition at due time. While moving on foot in the city they met a washer-man. They asked that person to give them some new clothes. But washer-man was Kansa's servant. Not only did he refuse them the clothes, he also abused the two brothers. So Krishna hit the evil washerman with his palm and split his head in two. Then the brothers selected the clothes of their choice. While Balaram dressed in blue Krishna chose yellow clothes to wear.

Then they wanted garlands to complete their adornment and so reached a garland-seller. The garland vendor thought as though these two were gods. And when the two brothers demanded flowers, not only did he give them the flowers but also worshipped them. Blessing the garland vendor, they went ahead.

While moving on the street they happened to meet a young woman who was exceptionally comely but she had a hump on her back. Her name was Kubja. She carried a salver of sandle-wood paste in her hands.

'For whom are you carrying this paste?' asked Krishna.

'This is for Kansa,' she replied "I am responsible for supplying this fragrant paste to the king.

But they forced her to give the paste which they rubbed on their body. In return to this paste Krishna jerked her body so straight by pressing her feet and putting pressure upwards by his hands on her jaws that her hump disappeared. With Kubja's body straightened and hump gone she became a flawless beautiful woman. Thanking Krishna she went home.

As they reached the main gate of the venue for the wrestling competition, they spotted a ferocious elephant (Kuvalyapuda) coming charging at them. The two brothers tackled the mad elephant with great agility and managed to slay it by throwing it away. As they entered the arena, they first spotted a huge bow kept on an altar which was to be worshipped. Krishna proceeded to tie a string to the bow which broke with a bang with his touch. The snapping of the bow was heard throughout the palace. The guards came and attacked the two brothers but the two managed to slay all the guards.

Since the two had entered the arena with much commotion, Kansa learnt about their arrival at the venue with quite a consternation. Nevertheless, he immediately asked Chanoor and Mushtik to go and wrestle with the two brothers and kill them.

When the competition began all earlier minor wrestlers were defeated by the two brothers with no difficulty. Then the final bout began in the main arena. The entire venue was very well decorated. There were ordinary seats for the common citizens and the special ones for the king and his guests. Kansa sat on the highest seat of all. The woman sat behind a partition.

With the echoing of the martial music the bout commenced. Chanoor and Mushtik stood in the middle of the ring flamboyanthy displaying their powerful muscles. The schedule was that Krishna was to take on Chanoor and Balrama on Mushtika. The first wrestling match between

Krishna and Chanoora began. It was a terrible bout. Both were strong and deft wrestlers. But eventually Krishna raised Chanoora's body aloft and whirled it around a hundred times before throwing Chanoora down on the ground. Chanoora met his instant death. Then Balarama took on Mushtik. He hit Mushtik's head with his fists and powerful punches. And then in a trick he grasped Mushtik so hard that Kansa's prized wrestler was strangulated to death.Meanwhile, Kansa sent another wrestler Toshalaka who was killed by Krishna in no time.

Seeing his prized fighters not only defeated but also slain Kansa became mad with rage. He yelled at the guards to capture the two brothers and tie them in Chains. But then Krishna let out a frightening laughter. He jumped up on the stage where Kansa was sitting and caught hold of the king by the latter's hair. He threw Kansa down on the ground who died on the impact. Then Krishna pulled the dead body so heavily on the ground that a deep pit was created. Eventually the body was thrown into the river Yamuna.

Kansa also had a brother called Sumati who came forward to avenge his brother's death. But Balarama killed him easily. Then Krishna and Balarama, held on the shoulders by the Jubiliant crowd, went to meet their parents Vasudeva and Devaki who were delighted to meet their long lost sons.

The vile Kansa had imprisoned the real king, his father Ugrasen. He was released and ceremonially restored to the throne. Indra, the chief of gods was delighted at the fall of Kansa. He presented a beautiful assembly hall, called Sudharma to Krishna who in turn gave it to the King Ugrasaen. Peace dawned there and people heaved a sigh of relief at the death of their tyrant ruler Kansa.

Since Kansa was now died, it was time the two brothers, Krishna and Balarama received formal education. So they were sent to their traditional guru, Sandipana's houses in Ujjayaini.[2] It took them only 64 days to receive all the education. Now, it was time the guru was given his traditional fees called 'Guru-Dakshina'. This fees the guru could demand in any form. Guru Sandipani had only one son who had died.

---

[2] Some versions claim the guru lived at Kachi.

Sandipani desired that as the Guru-Dakshina he wanted his son brought back to life.

Krishna and Balarama learnt that the guru's son was taken to the great ocean after death. So they took up their weapons and went to the ocean to demand their guru's son's dead body. The ocean told them that the son was actually with an 'asura' named Panchajana who had the form of a conch-shell. Krishna immediately entered into the depth of the ocean and killed the asura. From the skeleton of the daitya was made the conch-shell 'Panchajanya' which became Krishna's proud possession. He always blew it when heralding the advent of an important ocassion. Then the two brothers' repaired to Yama (death god's) Lok and defeated the deity to revive life in their guru's dead son. Then presenting that boy, alive, to the delighted guru in the form of the 'Gurudakshina' they went back to Mathura.

Jarasandha and Krishna

Jarasandha, the most powerful but a tyrant ruler was the king of Magadha and Kansa was his son-in-law. His two daughters named Asti and Prapti were married to Kansa. On hearing that Krishna had killed his son-in-law, Jarasandha raised a huge army and attacked Mathura, the seat of the Yadavas. He put the entire city under seize of his massive army.

Since Krishna, Baladeva (Balarama) and other Yadavas had only a few soldiers compared to Jarasandha's huge army, Jarasandha posed a big problem before them. Nevertheless, they still decided to fight against the Magadha King. At that time, from the sky a bow called Sharnga, two quivers that never ran out of arrows, and a mace named Kaumudi fell into Krishna's hands. For Balarama the weapons were a plough and a club named Sounanda. With these weapons the two brothers leading the Yadava clan managed to rout Jarasandha and he fled. But after only a few months the tyrant Magadha King again launched his ferocious attack but was again defeated. Although Jarasandha attacked them many a time, he couldn't defeat the Yadavas. However on Krishna's advice, later on, they migrated to Dwarika on the west coast to get rid of Jarasandha's attacks.

Kaliyavna and Krishna: There was a pious brahmana named Gargya in the assembly of the Yadavas. Once he was called 'impotent' by some Yadavas. This remark hurt the brahmana so much that he left for the southern ocean to perform a severe penance to propitiate Lord Shiv and get a boon of having a son. He wanted a son who could be scourge of the entire Yadava clan. He performed the penance with great devotion and ate only iron dust for food for 12 long years. At last, duly propitiated, Lord Shiva appeared before him and granted him the desired boon. After this a Yavana (foreigner) king came in contact with Gargya and pleased the brahmana as much as to make the latter allow him to copulate with his wife. Eventually a son with born to him with that Yavana king's contact with his wife. This son, black of hue, became the king of the Yavanas and owing to his black complexion came to be knwon as Kaliyavana (or black foreigner).

As he grew powerful he wanted to know from Narad about the powerful kings on the earth. He was told about the powerful clan of Yadava. So he decided to attack the yadavas. For this purpose he collected a huge army having thousands of chariots, horses, elephants and infantry. Then he made the massive army march towards Mathura to capture the Yadavas.

When Krishna heard about the Yavana army's march towards Mathura, he was very much worried. The threat from Jarasandha was still very much live. He realized that the Yadavas would become weakened from there war with Kaliyavana. And if Jarasandha's attack came after that, the Yadavas might even lose at the hands of Jarasandha. On the other hard of the Yadavas become weak from a war with Jarasandha, they would surely lose the bathe against Kaliyavana. Hence the prospect was very grim. It was, therefore, necessary to build a strong fort from where the Yadavas could wage a long drawn out war. With this idea Krishna went turned western shores of the ocean and requested the ocean to gave him13 Yojana of land for building a strong fort. The ocean, friendly to Krishna after the letter's endeavour to release his guru Sandipani's son gave him the land to build the city of Dwarika. There were many gardens and lakes in Dwarika. It was surrounded by walls and moats on all sides and there were several forts inside the city.

At Krishna's advice all the citizens of Mathura were brought to Dwarika which was well fortified.

Having secured his people Krishna decided to take on Kaliyavana single handedly. He started to play a dangerous 'hide and seek' game with Kaliyavana. Kaliyavana began to chase him, desirous of a fight. Krishna did so according to his well thought out plan. He knew about a powerful king called Muchukunda sleeping in a cave. That king, long ago had won a boon from the gods after his rendering major help to them against their fight with the demons which they eventually won, that whoever tried to disturb Muchukunda's sleep would be incinerated to ashes. So he entered the cave with Kaliyavana in hot pursuit of him. It was quite dark in the cave. Kaliyavana failed to make out as to who was sleeping inside the cave. He thought the sleeping person to be Krishna. Aggressively he forced the sleeping figure to wake up. As the enraged king Muchukunda looked at Kalyavana, the latter was instantly incinerated to ashes. All the while Krishna remained hiding in the cave. Having burnt up Kaliyavana king Muchukanda came out of the cave and found that people were now much shorter then they used to be. Deeming that Kaliyug must have made its advent, he left for doing his worship at Mount Gandhawadan. Subsequently, Krishna easily managed to defeat all the soldiers of Kaliyavana's army since they had nobody to guide them. This was how, by his sheer intelligence. Krishna got rid of the scourage of Yadava, the foreigner king Kaliyavana.

Balarama Turns the Course of the River Yamuna

Now since there was peace and quiet, Balrama thought of visiting Gokula and met his old friends. During his stay there he thoroughly enjoyed in the company of his friends.

One day while he was roaming about the place with his friends, he found that there was wine oozing out from Kadamb tree[3]. Balrama drank a lot of wine and became drunk. His body had become very hot because of that fluid's intoxicating effect. Since he had lost the control of his senses, in his sozzled state he asked the river to come close to

---

[3]Kadamb oozes a kind of fluid, which is highly intoxicating.

him as he wanted a cool bath "Change your course and come to me so that I may have bath in your cool waters, he said arrogantly.

But Yamuna ignored the instructions. This defiance made Balarama blew up in rage in his drunken stage. He took up his plough. With his plough he grasped the river's flow in such a way that it was forced to change its course and come close to Balarama. The river's course was eventually changed. Yamuna then appeared in a human form before Balarama and begged for forgiveness. Granting this, Balarama, the incarnation of the great serpent Shesh Nag, said: "Henceforth you shall continue to follow this course forever. Now I release your flow."

When Balarama's bath was over, Lakshami, the goddess of affluence appeared before him and gave him a garland of lotus which never fade. She also gave him two pieces of blue clothing. Balarama, then returned to Dwarika after having spent a couple of months in Gokula. There he married king Raivata's daughter Revati had two sons named Nishatha and Ulmuka. Balarama earned the epithet, 'Sankarshan' after he changed the course the river Yamuna.

Krishna's Marriage to Rukmini

King Bhishmaka was the ruler of the kingdom of Kundinpur. The king had a son called Rukmi and a daughter named Rukmini. The daughter Rukmini had heard so much about Krishna's handsomeness and achievements that she wanted to marry him. When Krishna heard about it he sent a formal proposal of marriage to Rukmini's father. But Rukmini's brother Rukmi was terribly against the Yadava, particularly Krishna. So he made his father refuse the proposal.

Bhishmaka, however, had good terms with Jarasandha. On his advice he decided to marry his daughter to Shishupal, another ally of Jarasandha. All these allies of Jarasandha went to Kundinpur to witness the 'Swayamvar' of Rukmini who was expected to chose Shishupal. The Yadava, along with Krishna were also invited to attend the ceremony. But a day before the marriage was due, Krishna, with connivance of his clan people, happened to abduct Rukmini who herself wanted nothing else.

Thereupon several kings — most of whom were Jarasandha's

allies — like Paundraka, Dantavakra, Viduratha, Shishupala, Jarasandha himself and Shalva attacked the Yadavas so as to capture Krishna. But Balaram and other Yadava managed to check their onslaught and allowed Krishna to escape with his abducted bride. However, Rukmi continued to chase the couple. Even though Rukmini had declared that her choice was only Krishna, Rukmi continued to pester them. Then Krishna defeated him easily along with his huge army. When Krishna was about to kill Rukmi, Rukmini said: "I have only one brother. Please spare his life!"

Although Krishna spared Rukmi's life, the arrogant prince didn't return to his kingdom. He had taken the resolve that he won't return to Kundinpur without Rukmini and without killing Krishna. So he stayed mid-way where he built a new city known as Bhojakata. He then twin settled there only.

Krishna, subsequently married Rukmini according to 'Rakshas' form of marriage. They had a son called Pradyumna who was kidnapped by Shambarasura as soon as he was born. However, later, on Pradyumna himself managed to slay Shambarasura.

Shambarasura and Pradyumna

Although the sage Parashar had only hinted about this story in the previous narration, on Maitreya's insistence he narrated it fully this way.

Shambarasura knew that Pradyumna was destined to kill him. So six days after Pradyumna's birth, he kidnapped the newly born son of Krishna — Pradyumna and threw him into the ocean. The ocean was full of dangerous aquatic beings. The baby might have died but a large fish swallowed him up. Later on, some fishermen caught the fish and brought it to Shambarasura!' kitchen.

Shambarasura had a house keeper named Mayawati. When the fish was cut, Mayawati found the baby inside. She was amazed: "Who is this boy and how did he come here?" she wondered. Then she sought the divine sage Narada to know about the origin of this boy. Then Narada enlightened her about Pradyumna. He also instructed her to bring up the boy properly.

This was what Mayawati proceeded to do. She was also well versed in the technique of casting magic spell (Maya) and other illusions. She told Pradyumna all about these when the boy grew up. Then she also told the boy about kidnapping by Shambarasura. Hearing this all, as Pradyumna became a little big, he challenged Shambarasure to a duel. Although Shambarasura used a lot of 'Maya' technique's, thanks to the knowledge Pradyumna had received from Mayawati, he could counter his every magic trick. Eventually he cast his own spell so thoroughly that Shambarasura was killed.

After this Pradyumna and Mayawati returned to Krishna and Rukmini. Everyone was happy and eventually Pradyumna married Mayawati.

Apart from Pradyumna, Krishna and Rukmini had eight other sons and a daughter. Krishna had seven other major wives apart from Rukmini. They were Kalindi, Mitra Vinda, Satya, Jambavati or Rohini, Sushila, Satyabhama and Lakshmana. Krishna had rescued many women also and when they were found to be shelter less. He married all of them. So, in all he had 16108 wives.

Pradyumna subsequently married King Rukmi's daughter and had a son named Aniruddha who had married Rukmi's grand daughter. On the occasion of this marriage all the Yadava chieftains including Krishna and Balarama had invited Rukmi's capital Bhojakata.

After the marriage, some kings who knew about Rukmi's animosity to the Yadava, advised Rukmi: "Balarama is addict to playing the dice although he can't play it well. Why not arrange a match of dice (gambling) so that you could defeat him easily?

Rukmi readily agreed to the proposition and soon a gambling session began between Rukmi and Balarama. In the first round, Rukmi won 4000 gold pieces off Balarama. This happened twice again as well. Seeing Balarama constantly losing the king of Kalinga and Rukmi began to laugh at Balarama. Balarama was furious and in a fit of rage placed four crores of gold pieces as a bet. Rukmi threw the dices but this time Balarama won.

'I have won,' exclaimed Balarama loudly. "No, you haven't" replied Rukmi laughtily."You did place the bet but I did not accept it. So you can't say that you've really won." Rukmi insisted.

However, then a divine voice from the sky gave its verdict that Balarama was the victor. Although verbally Rukmini had not accepted the bet, his throwing dices after Balarama's placing the bet did prove his accepting the bet. Though Rukmi did'nt accept this argument he couldn't have defied the divine verdict. But he did make an offensive remark Balarama's anger. He picked up a dices and threw it so forcefully at Rukmi that the latter died. Then Balarama also caught hold of the king of Kalinga and broke off his teeth which the king had exposed while laughing at Balarama earlier. Balarama grew so furious that he had killed many more other kings, who were friendly to Rukmi.

The Killing of Narakasur

Once the chief of the gods, Indra happened to visit Dwarika to give vent to his grievances against a mortal king Narakasura. This demoniac existence was the son of the Prithvi and the king of Pragjyotishpura. He was an oppressive ruler who loved troubling the people. He was a licher and was constantly kidnapping the daughter of all the weak kings of even gods and of the demons. After kidnapping and enjoying them he would imprison them in his fort. Narakasura had also stolen the umbrella of Varuna from which the rains came. The peak of Mount Mandara had also been stolen by him. So much so that he had the audacity of stealing the ear-ring's of the divine mother, Aditis and was now threatening to steal Indra's famous mount, the elephant Airavata.

Getting the request from Indra, Krishna decided to set Narakasura right. He thought of his famous mount as Vishnu, Garuda, and the bird immediately appeared before him. Then Krishna and Satyabhama rode on the Garuda and few towards Pragjyotishpura.

Near Pragjyotishpura, Narakasura had posted a demon guard called Munu who had installed many incisive stakes around the city wall to prevent its penetration. But that Lord (Krishna) quickly sliced off all the stakes with his famous disc Sudarshana. The Munu attacked him with his family. Krishna managed to slay all his 7000 sons and subsequently killed two others of them, named Hayagreeva and Panchajana to enter Pragjyotishpura.

Then a terrible war ensued between Narakasura and Krishna.

Eventually Krishna killed in thousands and thousands of the demon army soldiers and finally hacked Narakasura off in two parts with his mighty chakra.

When he entered Narakasura's 'herem' he found 16100 helpless, unsheltered women whom Narakasura had imprisoned to satiate his carnal lust. When released, all of them refused to go to their respectability places in the fear of their fathers, husbands and other relations rejecting them on the plea of their being defiled. So, out of pity Krishna married all of them to provide them a position of respectively in life. There were also several horses, elephants with four trunks and other valuable items. Krishna sent all of them to Dwarika. Krishna put the other divine things that Naraka had stolen on Garuda and then proceeded towards heaven to return them to their mightful owners.

The Tree Parijaat gets Transplanted in Dwarika

As Krishna and Satyabhama reached heaven astride their mount Garuda, Krishna blew his conch shell, Panchajanya, to announce his arrival. All the gods eagerly came out to welcome Krishna with Satyabhama in heaven. Krishna first went to Aditis to return his earrings which Narakasura had stolen. Aditi, the divine mother, was delighted and she blessed Satyabhama that henceforth she would remain perpetually young; that she would never grow old and ugly. Satyabhama gratefully accepted the boon.

Then Aditi instructed Indra to ritually worship Krishna and his spouse Satyabhama. But Shachi, Indra's wife, worshipped Satyabhama with ordinary flowers and not with Parijaat[4] flowers as was the divine custom, deeming Krishna's wife to be a mere mortal women. Satyabhama noticed the slight and felt offended. Later on when Krishna and Satyabhama went for a stroll in the divine gardens, they saw the Parijaat tree. Its leaves were of the copper color and the bark was of gold. Satyabhama was captivated by that tree and requested Krishna to take that tree to Dwarika. She became so enamoured of that tree that

---

[4]Erythrina Indica one of the five divine trees that exist in heaven.

she said: "If you really love me then please have this tree planted in our palace in Dwarika. I will wear this tree's flower on my hair as Shachi does.

Krishna laughingly complied with Satyabhama's request. He at once uprooted the tree and placed it on Garuda's back. However, the guards of heaven objected, saying: "Please don't take this precious tree. It belongs to Shachi." They also said that taking this tree this way might arouse the ire of the gods, particularly of Shachi. Satyabhama, already carrying a grudge against Shachi, blew up: "Who is Shachi and Indra to check up in taking this tree. Did it not originate from the sea churning? So everyone has a right to possess it. Why should it be deemed Shachi or Indra's personal property? You may go," she said to the guards," "and tell Shachi that my husband is taking this tree to Dwarika. She thought me to be a mere mortal women, didn't she? Now tall her to put all her divine powers to check its transfer to the mortal plains."

When the guards told Shachi about it she was furious. Incited by her, Indra attacked Krishna with all the gods, endowed with their weapon. Indra had his 'Vajra' (thunder bolt) and the others like Varuna, Agni etc also had their renowned clubs and spears, maces and swords. Indra led their offensive astrids his mount, Airavat. Seeing Indra approaching with aggressive intention, Krishna blew on his 'Panchajanya' and showered uncountable arrows on the divine army. The gods flung many weapons at him but Krishna skillfully nullified their impacts. Garuda also helped his master to taken on the gods. With a mace Krishna destroyed Yama's famous staff, with his chakra he smashed Varuna's nose alongwith the palanquin the god was seated in.With an askew glance Krishna robbed the sun of all shine. Even Agni's arrows were made ineffective. All the 'Vasus', 'Rudras' 'Maruts' and 'Gandharvas' that accompanied the gods had to flee in panic before Krishna's incomparable martial valour.

At least Krishna and Indra were locked in a duel while their mounts fought with each other in a fierce combat. Finally Indra readied his Vajra and Krishna took up his chakra. Everyone in the three worlds was frightened that these weapons clash might annihilates all the worlds. But when Indra hurled his Vajra, Krishna simply caught the weapon in his hand. He didn't fling his chakra in retaliation. Now Indra began to run in panic. Seeing him fleeing Satyabhama taunted: "O Mighty Lord of the gods, Why must you run scared? Aren't you Shachi's husband, the arrongant ruler of heaven? Fleeing this way like a coward dosen't behave you. Take back this Parijaat. Let the minds of the gods be at rest".

Then Indra apologised for all that happened. He also said that he was not ashamed of loosing to Krishna as Krishna was the incarnated form of Vishnu, the Supreme Lord. Krishna smiled and returned the Parijaat tree as well as Indra's Vajra. But while taking back his Vajra, Indra refused to take the tree back. He requested Krishna to take this tree to Dwarika and fulfil Satyabhama's wish. After Krishna's exist from the mortal world this tree would automatically return to heaven. So, taking along the divine tree Krishna and Satyabhama returned to Dwarika. The tree was planted in Krishna's palace. All the Yadavas came to behold it with unconcealed prides. Meanwhile all the wealth recovered from Narakasura's palace had also been stored in Dwarika which became the most affluent kingdom.

The Slaying of Dvivida

Dvivida was a monkey who was a fast friend of Narakasura and an enemy to the gods. Getting the news about Narakasura's death, this ape because much more belligerent to gods in sheer vengeance. In rage of losing his friend he started destroying all the yagyas that were performed by the sages and also prosecuted the sage in the murderous frenzy. He destroyed cities, villages and forest and started causing a chaos in the righteous order. He even uprooted the mountains and flung them into the oceans, causing flood due to over flowing of the oceans. He caused a serious threat to the entire established order.

One day he happened to reach before Balarama who was busy in drinking. Dvivida caused much disturbances there. He recklessly picked up Balarama's plough and club. Although repeatedly warned by Balarama he continued to laughed derisively at Balarama. This made up Balarama blew up in anger at the recalcitrant monkey. Balarama picked up his club and the ape also picked up a huge boulder to face him. Balarama broke the boulder to bits but then the ape began to hit him on the chest with his fits. At last Balarama cast a deadly blow by his clenched fist on the monkey's head and the ape died instantly. The gods were delighted at the ape's death and showered flowers on Balarama's out of sheer gratitude's for getting rid of that wile monkey.

The Vanasura Tale

Krishna had 16108 wives who together bore him more than eighty thousand sons. Best among them was Pradyumna whose son was Aniruddha.

Vanasura was Vali's son and he had a daughter named Usha. She was a devotee of Lord Shankar and Parvati. Once propitiated by her worship the divine couple had appeared before her. Then Usha asked goddess Parvati who her husband would be. Parvati replied: "In the (lunar) month of Vaishakh (Mid April to Mid May) a person would appear in her (Usha's) dream. That would eventually be your husband.

And this prediction vindicated itself in the coming months of Vaishakh. Usha did see a handsome youth in her dream but she had no idea about the identity of that person. She told about her dream to her friend Chitralekha. In order to identify the mysterious youth, Chitralekha started showing to usha various portraits of the handsome young personage of the reputed families coming from all categories: gods, Gandharvas and Kinnars. But the required person didn't figure in them. Then Chitralekha showed her the most handsome male youths among human species and Usha could easily identify Aniruddha.

Many years ago Vanasura had performed a devout penance to propitiats Lord Shankar and asked the deity to grant him occasion to fight with matching warriors. "I have ten thousand arms, Lord. What would I do if I fail to use them in fights." Vanasura pleaded. "Have patience". Lord Mahadeva advised him. "One day you will find your flag lying broken. When that happens, deem that you would soon be getting ample opportunities to fight with your 10,000 arms."

Vanasura was happy getting this boon from Lord Shankar.

Meanwhile, after identifying Usha's would be husband's identity Chitralekha wondered as to what she should do to get that person to her friend Usha. Then making her plan she went to Dwarika in disguise and secretaly eloped with Aniruddha with the help of her magic powers. Then she brought Aniruddha to Usha's palace. It was also the day when Vanasura found his flag lying broken. While he was thinking about this happening the guards came and informed him about Aniruddha's presence in Usha's palace. Immediately Vanasura sent his soldiers to fight with Aniruddha. But Aniruddha killed then all with a club.

Learning about this might adversary Vanasura himself entered the fray. Although initially he was beaten by Aniruddha, soon he cast his black magic spell to tie Aniruddha up in captivity.

Meanwhile the divine sage Narada, who has his unchecked access in entire universe, happened to reach Vanasur's palace and getting all the details went to tell Krishna, Balarama and all the Yadava about their son Aniruddha's fate. This information made Krishna, Balarama and Pradyumna along with other Yadava rush to rescue Aniruddha. The yadava forces led by Krishna came with such an aggressive thrust that they killed many enemy forces even before entering Vanasura's citadel. Vanasura also had a demon called Jwara who had a huge body, three arms and three legs. This demon had been born out of Mahadeva's body. Jwara was so powerful that he even caused Balarama some discomfort. But immediately Krishna created a demon from his body as well who killed the demon Jwara.

Then Krishna killed many demon soldiers. This made Vanasura himself jump the fray. Since Vanasura was Mahadeva's devotee, Mahadeva and Kartikeya also fought on Vanasura's side. So much so that Mahadeva's mount, Nandi, was the driver of Vanasura chariot. A terrible war between Krishna and Mahadeva ensued and everyone apprehended the end of the world owing to the threatened ferocity of the war. But Krishna managed to tire out Mahadeva, while Pradyumna scored over Kartikeya and Balarama killed thousands of Vanasura's soldiers. Then Vanasura confronted Krishna and hurled many arrows at Krishna. This onslaught made Krishna angry enough to hurl his famous Sudarshana Chakra which sliced off Vanasura's all arms. But before Krishna could kill Vanasura Mahadeva intervened and begged for Vanasura's life. Krishna acceded to the request of Mahadeva. Then Usha and Aniruddha's marriage was formally solemnized and the yadavas returned to Dwarika with the new bride for their most prominent scion.

The Slaying of Paundraka, the Pseudo 'Incarnation of Lord Vishnu'

Paundraka was a king who suffered from the illusion that he was the real incarnation of Lord Vishnu on earth. He had even adopted the name 'Vasudeva' and once sent a messenger to Krishna with the warning: "Stop pretending yourself to be incarnation of Lord Vishnu. It is I who am that divine being's human form. If you want to be safe and happy, you must come to me and apologise for the pretension."

Krishna was amused getting this message. Then he also learnt that Paundraka was the friend of king of Kashi. Krishna told the messanger that he would be soon going to Kashi and Panudraka might meet him there. Getting the message, Paundraka got ready with his army. As Krishna arrived in Kashi on his mount Garuda, Paundraka with his army came charging at him. But using his renowned weapons with great skill, Krishna not only killed many soldiers of Paundraka but also the Pseudo-Vasudeva, himself with his Sudarshana Chakra. He cast the fatal blow with his mace named Kaumudi. In that confrontation, Paundraka's friend, the ruler of Kashi was also killed. Krishna not only sliced the Kashi ruler's head with his Chakra but had it gibbeted on the main gate of Kashi. Then Krishna returned to Dwarika.

When the people of Kashi found their king's head at the main gate, they were rather amazed. Soon the king of Kashi's son found that Krishna was responsible for this. So he devotedly prayed to Mahadeva who appeared before him. Then the son of the slain Kashi ruler requested the empress god in creates such a demon as might kill Krishna who murdered his father. The Lord created a 'Kritya' (a demon with a charged spell) and asked it to do whatever Kashi ruler's son said. The demon started for the mission and entered Dwarika.

When Krishna found that demon coming to him with a murderous intention, he hurled his Sudarshan chakra. The demon was nervous and fled back to Kashi. But chasing the demon, the Chakra not only destroyed the demon, the son of the Kashi ruler but entire army of Kashi and the whole of city. Then it quickly returned to his master, Krishna.

Samba's Wedding

Samba, the son of the Krishna wanted to marry Duryodhan's daughter. Once when she was moving alone, he kidnapped her. However, Karna, Duryodhana, Drona and other warrions of the Kaurava challenged Samba and eventually managed to imprison him. When the Yadavas learnt about Samba's imprisonment they readied their forces and left ford Hastinapur.

But Balarama restrained the Yadavas saying "Leave this problem to me. I'll go alone and talk to Duryodhan. He has been my disciple. I hope he will listen to me and release Samba."

With this intention Balarama left for Hastinapur but did not enter the city. He only sent the message of his arrival, hearing which Duryodhan and all other's came to pay their respect to Balarama. Then Balarama told the purpose of his arrival," My king Ugrasena has asked me to convey this message. Please pardon Samba and release him." However, the Kauravas were unwilling to do so. They counter questioned Balarama: "How dare your king order us this way? Samba had committed a serious offence. He has tried to attack the dignity of the Kauravas clan. He must suffer for this tell your Ugresena that we are not his subjects."

With this point blank refusal, the Kauravas returned to Hastinapur. Balarama was furious. "They (the Kauravas) seem to have become rather hot-headed. While I am requesting they are behaving in this arrogant manner." And then enraged Balarama grasped the foundations of Hastinapur city with his plough and prepared to hurl the whole city into the Ganga. When Hastinapur's foundation began to shake the Kauravas come to their senses. They rushed to Balarama begging his forgiveness. He asked them to bring Samba and his wife to him. Getting Samba released with his newly married wife, Balarama returned to Dwarika after forgiving the Kuravas. It is believed that ever since that day Hastinapur seemed to lean towards the river on one side.

The End of The Yadava Clan: After the bloody war of Mahabharata, the Yadava's clan was a divided lot. Some still favoured the Kauravas while other supported the Pandavas cause Kritaverma led one group and the other group was led by Satyaki. With the result, their squabbles became an every day affair. Although Krishna tried to pacify them, he didn't succeed much.

One day the Yadavas assembled in a place of pilgrimage near Dwarika called Pindarika. Some delinquent Yadava Youth drank to the gills and in their sozzled state they tried to make fool of the sages Kanva, Vishwamitra and Narada. They dressed up Samba as though he was a pregnant woman. Then they brought the 'lady' before the sages and asked: "O great Sages! Tell us whether this woman will deliver a son or a daughter." The sage Kanva saw through their mischief. Enraged at this insult, the sage declared angrily: "This person will give birth to an iron club", the sages further said: "And this will destroy your entire clan".

As predicated, in due course a club came out of Samba's body. When king Ugrasena heard about the curse, releasing the veracity of the sages curse, he had the club totally pulverised and scattered on the ocean nearby. However, the particles of the dust got changed into sharp reeds that grew on the shores of the ocean. A part of that club which couldn't be pulverised had sunken in the ocean but a fish managed to swallow it. Later on when the fish was caught by a fisherman, it emerged out of it when the fish's stomach was priced open. The fisherman threw it casually on the ground which was eventually gathered by a hunter called Jara who fashioned the iron piece as the pointed blade of his one arrow.

Meanwhile, on a holy occasion all the Yadavas gathered around a place of pilgrimage on the holy mount in the Prabhas Kshetra. Only one Yadava, Uddhava didn't go to attend the ceremony at Prabhas Kshetra as he had left for doing his devoted penance on the Mount Gandhamadan. In Prabhas, much against the custom the Yadavas began to drink and indulge in obscene pranks. Soon they lost their senses. They started to fight among themselves and picked up the reeds that were growing on the shores as weapons. Though Krishna did try to control the berserk Yadavas, they paid no heed to Krishna's advice. Then deeming the approaching extinction of the Yadavas as the will of the destiny, Krishna withdrew to a quiet corner on the shore with his chariot driver, Daruka. Meanwhile, the Yadavas fought with each other to cause the extinction of their clan. Balarama had also left the fighting arena and retired to a quiet Banyan. While moving around the shore Krishna and Daruka found

Balarama, the incarnation of the Shesh-Naga the serpent that is failed to support the earth-seated under the tree with a huge white coloured snake emerging out of Balarama's mouth and disappearing into the ocean. This signified Balarama quitting his mortal coil.

Seeing this, Krishna told Daruka: "Now you go and tell King Ugrasena about all this. Soon I would be also quitting my mortal coil and then the sea will swallow up the whole city of Dwarika barring my dwelling place. That place will remain intact to help my devotees seek my blessings when I am gone. So you tell everyone left in Dwarika to leave after Arjuna's arrival. Then you inform Arjuna all that happened here and request him to take all the women to Dwarika to safety. My great grand son Vajra should be appointed the king after this catastrophe."

Daruka paid his last respects to Krishna and departed to inform the persons Krishna had ordered him to. Then Krishna laid down with one foot placed on the knee of the other to reflect in meditation. About this time the hunter Jara was looking for his prey. From a distance he thought as if a deer was standing at a distance whereas what he had observed was the reddened sole of Krishna's raised foot. The hunter Jara then took out the same arrow whose top had the iron piece moulded as the pointed blade and shot the arrow aiming at the target. It hit Krishna's sole and the Great Lord quitted his mortal coil. When he reached near the target Krishna was conscious. The hunter begged forgiveness as he had hurt Krishna unknowingly. Krishna assured him that he (Jara) would go to heaven. As Krishna's soul left for Baikuntha, a chariot immediately arrived to take Jara to heaven. Krishna was mortally 125 years of age when he quitted his body.

When Arjuna got Krishna's last message he was shocked. Eventually as advised by Krishna he came to Dwarika and with due ceremony performed the funeral rites of all the Yadavas including Krishna and Balarama. Krishna's eight major wives and Balarama's Revati preferred to sit on the burning pyre of their husbands dead bodies and ended their life. Ugrasena, Devaki and Vasudeva also ended their life by entering a raging fire. The remaining ladies of Dwarika left with Arjuna towards Hastinapur.

But curiously enough, the famed archer, the mighty Arjuna failed to protect them when their caravan was attacked mid-way by the tribal (Bheela) dacoits. Arjuna found him totally powerless despite his still having the Gandeeva bow. He seemed to have lost all his strength and knowledge with Krishna's exit from this world. The Yadava ladies, with much difficulty, managed to reach Mathura on their own, surviving the dacoits onslaughts. Since then Mathura has become the home of the helpless widows.

Meanwhile, as soon as Krishna left for Baikuntha, the Parijaat tree and the assembly hall named 'Sudharma' returned to heaven. The exit of Krishna made it clear that Kaliyug had already set in. Dwarika was swallowed up by the sea with the exception of the palace in which Krishna lived.

Reaching Hastinapur, a baffled Arjuna asked the sage Vedvyas. "O Sage? How I became so powerless as to lose battle to those aboriginal dacoits?" Vedvyas said: "Your source of power only Krishna. Now he is gone so you lost all your power! Hearing this the disappointed Pandavas left for the Himalayas after appointing Parikshit as the ruler of Hastinapur.

The Advent of Kaliyuga

When requested by Maitreya sage Parashar told him about the changes that would occur when Kaliyug sets in.

In Kaliyug, the norms of 'Varna' and 'Ashrama' would not be followed as laid down in the Vedas. No one will pray to the gods. Congenial relations between the 'Guru and Shishya' will cease. 'Might is right' would be an accepted dictum. Women will care more for their external beauty. Wealth will be accorded the top priority in all human endeavours. People won't care for Dharma and be devoted to acquiring material possessions. Greedily they would spend money for their own pleasures and not for looking after the guests. Money earning will become the chief mission of all and no attention would be paid whether it is earned through fair or foul names.

Men would, by nature be dirty and they won't bathe before having their meals. Physically the human stature will progressively decrease.

Women will not obey their husbands. The kings will be tyrants and they will oppress subjects for personal gains. Taxes will be imposed recklessly, People will age very soon and their life span will be considerably curtailed. Evil will flourish with no one worshipping Vishnu. All classes will behave like the Shoodras.

However, there would be one advantage in Kaliyug. In Satyayuga one had to do a lot of 'Tapasya' to earn a little Punya (merit) but in Kaliyug a little 'Tapsaya' will yield tremendous 'Punya'. The equivalent scale is like this: ten years of Tapasya in Satya-Yuga are equal to one year of Tapsaya in Treta Yug, one month Tapsaya in Dwapar Yuga and one day of Tapasya is Kali age.

Vyasdeva said that Shoodra and women could acquire Punya easily. They have only to serve other classes and their male folks respectively to earn great merit in Kaliyug while the Brahmanas and other classes would have to follow their Dharmas religiously to earn even a bit of merit.

The Types of Pralaya or Dissolution

Although details of Pralaya have already described in the preceeding pages their various categories are being described now.

There are three types of Pralaya. First being 'Brahma' or 'Naimittika' which takes place at the end of the Kalpa i.e.,after one of Brahma's days and when 14 Manus have reigned. Before this Pralaya the earth becomes very weak and there are no rains for a hundred years. Vishnu, in Rudra form drinks up all the water of the rivers, oceans and other sources. Then seven rays of the sun manifest themselves as seven different sons. These scorching suns burn up all the realms. Then thick dark clouds of rain pour water continously as much as to drown all the land. It becomes dark every where. For a hundred years the winds blow ferociously. All this while Vishnu sleeps on the waters till the worlds are created afresh.

The second type of Pralaya is called Prakritika Pralaya. The perfect balance of the three basic gunas (Sattvik, Rajasik and Tamasik) is called Prakriti.At the time of Pralaya when Prakriti becomes assimilated in 'Paramatman' (Supreme Being) this is called Prakritika Pralaya in which all the three gunas become totally seperate and the world is reduced to its elemented form. The third type of Pralaya is called 'Atyalika Pralaya' divine This refers to the three types of distress: Adhyatmika (or spiritual), Adhidaivika (beyond the divine and Adhibhantika (beyond the elemental order). The first distress consists of physical and mental discomforts as also astral; the second due to the elementals imbalance and third due to adverse interaction among the beings, such as snakes or ghosts. At the 'Atyantika Pralaya''all these distress also disappear or they lose their ordered sequence.

Why the Yadava Women Suffered at the Hands of the Dacoits

When Arjuna had asked the sage Vyas about the reason behind the Yadava women suffering at the hands of the Bhila dacoits, Vyas ji told him that this was their destiny. In fact all the Yadava women were Apsaras in the earlier lives. Once they were making merry with gods after the gods victory over the demons. They happened to find the sage Ashtavakra doing his worship while placed in knee-deep water. Seeing his devotion the Apsaras bowed to the sage who gave them the boon that they would get their desired husbands. But as the sage came out of water, seeing his malformed[5] body the Apsaras couldn't hide their smile. With the result, the sage was angry and said that in next life they would suffer disgrace for their ill-manners However, later on, when requested, the sage modified his curse by saying that even after suffering disgraces they would go to their chosen abode. Concluding the sage Vyas said: "Arjuna! Don't brood over this happening. The wise accept the rule of providence with total respect. Now your period on the earth is over, so by making Parikshita the king, you brothers should also go to the Himalayas."

The Tale of Keshidhwaja and Khandikya

This is the tale of two brothers, one of whom wanted to acquire spiritual knowledge and other the knowledge through Karma (Action). The moral of this story is that spiritual knowledge is superior to the knowledge acquired through Karma. Keshidhawaja eventually told

---

[5]Sage Ashthavakra had his peculiar body having eight unwanted contortions.

Khandikya about the true knowledge which means knowledge of the 'Atman' which is different from mere physical body. True knowledge was that which taught that the 'Atman' was part of the 'Paramatman' and that one should therefore not get attached to material or mortal possession. This realization that man is more than body comes through only yoga which means uniting the 'Atman' with 'Paramatman'.

The Descent of the Puranas From Their Origin To Us

E ons ago Brahma, the creator, himself had told the sage Ribhu the story of the Puranas. From Ribhu the knowledge passed to Priyavarta who passed it to Bhaguni. Bhaguni imparted it to Staramitra who gave it to Dadheechi. From Dadheechi it passed to Sarasvata who gave it to Bhrigu. Bhrigu passed it on to Puruputsa who gave it to Narmada. Narmada gave it to Dhritarashtra and Poorana who passed it on to Vasuki from whom it went to Vatsa. Vatsa gave it to Ashvatara who recited these stories to Kambala and Kambala gave this knowledge to Iravata. From him these Puranas (the ancient records) reached the Patal-loka (nether world). From there Vedashiri recovered the knowledge and passed it on to Paramati who gave it to Jastukarna. It was Jatukarna who recited these stories to noble persons, holy sages and other deserving people. I (sage Parashara) had heard it in my previous life from Saraswata Muni (seer). Owing to a boon that I had received from sage Pulastya. I happened to remember it and now I have narrated to you. You shall be reciting these Puranas to Shamak rishi at the end of the Kali Age", concluded sage Parashara.

Those who listen to their Pauranic stories with rapt attentions find Lord Vishnu propitiated easily. With the result, they have their all wishes fulfilled by Vishnu's grace. Not only that the Lord also help them in discharging their mortal duties as well. The result of listening to these Puranas is that those who do so achieve some rare feats in all the three worlds. That is not achievable by any other endeavour in this mortal world. It is so because Lord Vishnu is he base of this entire creation. Hence their listening snaps all the bondage of this transistory existence while fulfilling all ambitions, aspirations and provides the listener with an immense bliss.

Thousand Names of Lord Vishnu

Lord Vishnu's thousand names or 'Vishnusahastranam' has great significance for a devotee of the Lord Bheeshma, the legendary Grand uncle of the Kaurav and the Pandavas. While instructing Yudhisthir before he quit his mortal frame, he says in the 'Mahabharat' that chanting the thousand names of Lord Vishnu is the most effective Incantation or Mantra to ensure all kinds of happiness, pleasure and bliss to the chanter by the Grace of Lord Vishnu, not only in this world, but also in the next. For the benefit of the curious reader, the brief meaning of these names has also been given alongside.

1:	Vishwam:	The cause of the happening of the world.
2:	Vishnu:	All pervading.
3:	Vashatkār:	The object of the Vashat worship in the Yagya.
4:	Bhootabhavya bhavatprabhu:	Master of the past, present and future.
5:	Bhootakrita:	The creator of the physical World.
6:	Bhootabhrita:	The Sustainer of the world (physical).
7:	Bhāvah:	Eternal and Self-created.
8:	Bhootātma:	The Dwelling spirit in every being's soul.
9:	Bhootabhāvan.	The Creator and Sustainer of the Physical World.
10:	Pootātma:	The soul Purified.
11:	Paramātma:	The Supreme Spirit.
12:	Muktānām Paramā : Gatih	The ulitimate stage of the Liberated Soul.
13:	Avyayah:	Imperishable.
14:	Purushah:	Dweller in the Pur (body).
15:	Sakshee:	Witness to all happenings.
16:	Kshetragya:	He who knows all about the body and its nature.
17:	Akshārah:	Undecayable.
18:	Yogah:	The summit combination of mind and body.
19:	Yogavidām Neta:	The leader Who Knows Yoga.
20:	Pradhān purusheshwar:	The Master of Nature and Being.
21:	Nārasim havapuh:	Man-Iion bodied.

22:	Shreemān:	He who holds Lakshmi close to his bosom.
23:	Keshava:	Symbolising the Trinity with Brahma representing(Ka), Vishnu(ā), Mahadeva (Ish).
24:	Purushottam:	The Best Among the Decayable and Undecayble bodies.
25:	Sarvah:	All in All.
26:	Sharvah:	The Destroyer of the Creation (at Dissolution).
27:	Shivah:	The Auspicious Form, beyond the three Attributes.
28:	Sthānu:	Stable.
29:	Bhootadi:	The root cause of all beings.
30:	Nidhirvyayah:	The Imperishable embodiment of the bodily form surving through the Dissolution.
31:	Sambhavah:	Emerging at will.
32:	Bhāvanah:	The Bestower of Fruit of Actions.
33:	Bharta:	The Sustainer of the World, who gives food etc. to Beings.
34:	Prabhavah:	The Special (Divine) Existence.
35:	Prabuh:	The Lord of All.
36:	Ishwar:	The Lord of All Opulence.
37:	Swayambhoo:	The Self-Created Lord.
38:	Shambhuh:	The Bestower of Bliss to the Devotees.
39:	Āditya:	The son of mother Aditi.
40:	Pushkarāksha:	The Lotus Eyed.
41:	Mahāswanah:	One who is beyond life and death.
43:	Dhātā:	The Carrier of All.
44:	Vidhātā:	The Creator of deeds and their fruits.
45:	Dhaturuttamah:	The Creator of the best deeds and their effect.
46:	Aprameyah:	Not Proveable by evidence etc.
47:	Hrisheekeshah:	The Master of Senses.
48:	Padmanābhah:	Having lotus in the Navel from which originated Creation.
49:	Amaraprabhu:	The Master of the celestials.
50:	Vishwakarma:	The Creator of the whole world.
51:	Manuha:	The progenitor.
52:	Twashta:	The Cause of decay in all beings at the time of Pralaya or Dissolution.

53:	Sthavishtha:	Huge-bodied.
54:	Sthaviro Dhruvah:	Very Ancient and Very Stable.
55:	Agrihāhya:	Incomprehensible fully by mind.
56:	Stāshwatah:	Eternal.
57:	Krishnah:	Drawing everyone's attention forcibly by his Extreme Beauty: Lord Krishna.
58:	Lohitaksha:	The Red-Eyed.
59:	Pratardanah:	Destroyer of Beings at the time of Dissolution.
60:	Prabhootah:	Well endowed with knowledge, opulence and virtues.
61:	Trikakbhh dadhām:	The Support of Top, Middle and Bottom Quarters (Directions).
62.	Pavitram.	All purifie.
63:	Mangalam param:	Supremely Auspicious.
64:	Ishaanah:	The Controller of all Spirits.
65:	Prānadah:	The Giver of life.
66:	Jyeshtha:	The Eldest (among all).
67:	Shreshtha:	The Best.
68:	Prajāpati:	The Sustainer of All Being; the progenitor.
69:	Hiranyagarbha:	Permeating like life in the primal Aurum Ovam.
70:	Pranah:	Life-force of every being.
71:	Bhoogarbhah:	The Sustainer of Earth in its Embryonic stage.
72:	Mādhavah:	The Master of Goddess Lakshmi.
73:	Madhusoodanah:	The Slayer of the Demon Madhu.
74:	Ishah:	Omnipotent Lord.
75:	Vikrami:	Chivalrous.
76:	Dhanvi:	Wielder of the Bow Sharnga.
77:	Medhāvee:	Precocious.
78:	Vikramah:	The Order-Setter
80:	Anuttamah:	Peerless.
81:	Durādharsha:	Unassailable.
82:	Kritagya:	Grateful {who reqards greatly for even very little effort in his worship}.
83:	Kritiha:	The Motivating force in the Being's Efforts.
84:	Atmavān:	Reposed in His Own Glory. {The Konwer of self}.

85:	Sureshah:	The Lord of the gods.
86:	Sharanam:	The Shelter of All.
87:	Sharm:	The form of the Supreme Being.
88:	Vishwareta:	The cause of the World.
89:	Prajābhavah:	The Progenitor of All Beings.
90:	Ahah:	The Light-form.
91:	Samvatsarah:	The Setter of Time-Cycle.
92:	Vyālah:	He-like a Serpent-no body could hold Him.
93:	Pratyaya:	Comprehensible only to the Best Brain.
94:	Sarvadarshanah:	The Seer of All.
95:	Adah:	Beginning Less.
96:	Sarveshwarah:	The God of all gods.
97:	Siddha:	Ever evident.
98:	Siddhi:	The Net Result of All.
99:	Sarvādih:	The root cause of all beings.
100:	Acchyuta:	Infallible.
101:	Vrishākapi:	Like the Bull and Monkey or the Dharma and its tenets; also like the Bull and Boar.
102:	Ameyātma:	Indefinable Body.
103:	Sarvayogavinihstratah:	Comprehensible by scores of means, ordained by the Scriptures.
104:	Vasuh:	The Abode of All Beings.
105:	Vasumanah:	Large Hearted.
106:	Satyah:	The Truth.
107:	Samātma:	The Spirt Dwelling Evenly Among All Beings.
108:	Asammitah:	Immeasurable.
109:	Samah:	Equinamous.
110:	Amogh:	Unerring.
111:	Pundereekakhshah:	The One Having Lotus Like eyes.
112:	Vrishakarma:	The Doer of the Deeds to Sustain Dharma.
113:	Vrishākriti:	The Bull-like form (of Dharma).
114:	Rudrah:	He who Removes the cause of Sorrow.
115:	Bahushira:	The One with Many Heads.
116:	Babhruha:	The Nourisher of the Realms.
117:	Vishwayoni:	The Origin of the World.
118:	Shuchishrava:	The one with Noble Glory.
119:	Amritah:	Immortal.
120:	Shāshwat-sthanu:	Ever lasting and Stable.

121: Vararoha:	The High Rider.
122: Mahatapah:	Manifestative form (result) of the Great penance.
123: Sarvagah:	The All-pervading Cause.
124: Sarvavidbhanu:	The All-Konwing Enlightenment.
125: Visvaksenah:	The Pulveriser of the Demonic forces merely by the preparation to fight.
126: Janardanah:	The Destroyer of peoples' (devotees) distress.
127: Vedah:	The Manifested learinng-the veda-form.
128: Vedavita:	One who knows the real meaming of the Vedas.
129: Avyangah:	Perfect in every sense, or He who has nothing that is imperfect.
130: Vedangah:	Who has vedas as His Body Parts (i.e; the ultimate fount of Knowledge).
131: Vedagya:	The knower of the Vedas.
132: Kavi:	The poet (Knowing every thing).
133: Lokadhyaksha:	Master of All Realms.
134: Suradhyaksha:	The Head of gods.
135: Dharmadhyaksha:	The Head of the Dharma; the one who decides what is Dharma and Adharma or what is noble and What is iniquitous.
136: Kitakrita:	He who does action without cause.
137: Chaturatma:	The spirit of the four pronged world.
138: Chaturvyooha	The four arrays of life: Creation, sustenance, destruction and survival.
139: Chaturbhuja:	The four Armed (Lord Vishnu).
140: Chaturandrishta:	The four-jawed form (of Lord Narasimha).
141: Bhrajishnu:	Uniformly radiant form.
142: Bhojanam:	The nourishment (Provider to the devotees).
143: Bhokta:	The Sufferer in the form of Porush (Being) of punishment and Enjoyer of the rewards.
144: Sahishnu:	Tolerant.
145: Jagadadijah:	self-originating Primal Aurum ovam-the root of the world.
146: Anaghah:	The Sinless.
147: Vijaya:	The Excellor in all matches.

148:	Jeta:	A Natural Victor.
149:	Vishwayoni:	The Procreator of the world.
150:	Punarvasu:	The Spirit which repeatedly comes back to the body.
151:	Upendra:	The younger brother of Indra.
152:	Vāman:	Incarmating Vāman (the Dwarf).
153:	Pranshu:	Growing very high to jump across all the three realms.
154:	Amogha:	One Who does not make futile attempts.
155:	Shuchi:	The Purifier (to all by his worship).
156:	Urjita:	Supremely Energised.
157:	Ateendra:	Excelling over Indra in the self-knowledge.
158:	Sangrah:	One who collects everything at the time of Dissolution (Pralaya).
159:	Sargah:	The Cause of the Creation.
160:	Dhritātma:	Beyond the cycle of life and death, the one who creates Himself at will.
161:	Niyamah:	The One Who Brings Ordar in Creator.
162:	Yamah:	The Controlling Deity Inside every being.
163:	Vedya:	Approachable by those who seek their welfare.
164:	Vaidya:	Well versed in all Knowledge.
165:	Sadayogi:	Ever reposing in the yoga.
166:	Veerahā:	Slayer of the demons for protecting Dharma.
167:	Mādhava:	The Lord of All Konwledge.
168:	Madhu:	The Delighter of every heart like nectar.
169:	Ateendriya:	Beyond the approach of senses.
170:	Mahamayah:	The Great Illusor.
171:	Mahotsāha:	Ever enthusiastic to create, sustain and Dissolute the world.
172:	Mahābalah:	Supremely Powerful.
173:	Mahābuddhi:	Supremely Wise.
174:	Mahāveerya:	Supremely Valorous.
175:	Mahāshakti:	Supremely Competent.
176:	Mahadyuti:	Supremely Radiant.
177:	Anirdeshyavapu:	Of Undefineable Image.
178:	Mahdridhrika:	He who supported the mount Madar at the time of churning the ocean for getting nectar as also the Govardhan (in

	His Krishnā Form) for protection of cows.
179: Maheshvāsa:	Weilder of a Great Bow.
180: Maheebharta:	The Giver of food to earth.
181: Sreeman:	One endowed with oppulence
182: Ameyatma:	Immeasurable Being
183: Shreeniwas:	The Abode of Lakshmi.
184: Satāngati:	The final Refuge of the noble.
185: Aniruddha:	Indomitable without true devotion.
186: Surānanda:	The Delighter of gods.
187: Govindah:	Comprehensible through the Vedas study.
189: Mareechi:	The Radiance of the radiant.
190: Daman:	The queller of the delinquence.
191: Hamsa:	The Swan whom He Created to enlighten Brahma.
192: Suparna:	Master of Garuda who has beautiful wing.
193: Bhujagottam:	The best among the serpents, Sheshanag.
194: Hiranyanabha:	One having aureate navel for the creation of the world.
195: Sutapah:	On who performs right penances.
196: Padmānabh:	One having a lotus in His navel.
197: Prajāpati:	Lord of all creation.
198: Amrityu:	The One Without Death.
199: Sarvadrika:	One who sees all.
200: Sinha:	Destroyer of the wicked.
201: Sandhātā:	One who brings efforts and rewards together.
202: Sandhimān:	One who fills the gap between the effor and the result.
203: Sthir:	Immutable.
204: Aja:	One who cleanses His devotees' heart from vices.
205: Durmarshan:	Whose (dazzling) radiance is unbearable.
206: Shasta:	Ruler over all.
207: Vishrutātmā:	Renowned in the Scriptures.
208: Surāriha:	Slayer of the gods' enemies.
209: Guru:	Teacher of all.
210: Gurutam:	The Greatest Teachar.
211: Dhām:	The final refuge of all.
212: Satya:	True Being.
213: Satya Parākram:	One who performs real feats.

214: Nimisha:	Whose eyers are closed in the yoga-meditation.
215: Animish:	Who Incarnated in the fish form.
216: Sragvee:	One who dons Vaijayanti garland.
217: Vāchaspati: Rudāradhee	The Master of All Knowledge that reveals the Reality.
218: Agranee:	Who Moves in the Vanguard (and take the aspirant to final release).
219: Grāmani:	Leader of a group.
220: Shreemān:	One with all glory and opulence.
221: Nyayah:	The argument in logic proved by facts.
222: Neta:	The Driver (of the world in the form of a vehicle)
223: Sameeran:	Permeating the whole world like air.
224: Sahastra moordhā:	A Thousand headed.
225: Sahastrāksha:	A Thousand Eyed.
226: Vishwatma:	The spirit of the world.
227: Sahastrapādā:	One with thousand feet.
228: Āvartan:	One who keeps this global cycle moving.
229: Nivrittātma:	The Released Soul.
230: Samvrat:	Enveloped by His own Illusion
231: Sampramardan:	Crushing every one is His Rudra form.
232: Ahahsamvartak:	One who begins the day or year (in the form of the sun).
233: Vahni:	The fire which accepts all offering (in a sacrifice).
234: Anilah:	The wind in the form of vital air.
235: Dharanidhar:	Supporter of the Earth (In the form of the Boar and the Serpent).
236: Suprasād:	Gracious to even the wicked (by granting space in His Abode after slaying their bodies).
237: Prasannātma:	The Delighted soul.
238: Vishwadhrik:	The Support of the World.
239: Vishwabhuk:	The Nourisher of the world.
240: Vibhuha:	All Pervading.
241: Satkartā:	Hospitable to His devotees.
242: Satkrita:	Adorable by those worshipped.
243: Sādhu:	One who Make the Devotees achieve their aim.
244: Jahnu:	One who destroys beings at the time of Dissolution.

245: Nārāyanah:	One who reposes in water, Or, Water is whose home, or Abode.
246: Narah:	One who guides the noble.
247: Asankheya:	He who can't be represented by figures.
248: Aprameyaatmā:	Immeasurable by any scale.
249: Vishistah:	Especial, exquisite.
250: Shistakrita:	Who controls all.
251: Shuchi:	Supremely pious.
252: Siddhartha:	He who has succeded in his mission.
253: Siddhasankalpah:	One with resolute determination.
254: Siddhidah:	Bestower rewards according to the doers efforts.
255: Siddhi sādhan:	He who provides means for accomplishment.
256: Vrishāhi:	Reposing the effects of the sacrifice (Yagya) like Dwadasha and others within his control.
257: Vrishabhah:	One who showers choicest gifts for his devotees.
258: Vishnuh:	Embodiment of nobility.
259: Vrishaparva:	The stairs of Dharma to seek salvation for the aspirants.
260: Vrishodar:	Holding the Dharma close to heart.
261: Vardhan:	One who ensures prosperity to His devotees.
262: Vivaktah:	One who remains aloof from the world.
263: Shrutisagar:	An ocean of Vedic knowledge.
264: Subhujah:	Of well formed arms (for protecting the world).
265: Durdharah:	He who can't be supported by anyone.
266: Vardhaman:	He who grows life in the world.
267: Vāgmi:	The originator of the Vedic speech.
268: Mahendra:	Lord of Lords.
269: Vasudah:	Bestower of wealth.
270: Vasuh:	The Embodiment of riches.
271: Naikaroopah:	In Myriad forms.
272: Vrihadroopah:	The Universal form.
273: Shipavishtah:	The Radiance in the sun rays.
274: Prakāshan:	One who Illumines everything.
275: Ojastejodyutidhar:	One who has vitality, shine and radiance.
276: Prakāshatma:	The Enlightened Soul.

277:	Pratapan:	Providing Heat to all luminaries like sun and fire.
278:	Riddha:	Well versed in Dharma, Knowledge etc.
279:	Spashtākshar:	With well defined letter (word) like 'AUM'.
280:	Mantra:	Comprehended by hymns of Rig, Sām and Yajur vedas.
281:	Chandrānshu:	Like cool moonlight to the nobles distrersed with mundane heat.
282:	Bhaskardyuti:	Radiant like the sun.
283:	Amritānshoodbhava:	The origin of the moon, the sea, at the time of churning.
284:	Bhanuh:	He who gives light to see.
285:	Shashbindu:	Like the moon-with the rabbit sign in the heart-to rear up the world.
286:	Sureshwar:	Lord of the gods.
287:	Aushadhim:	The Medicine to cure all worldly ills.
288:	Jagatah-Setu:	The bridge to go across this world.
289:	Satyadharma parat : kramah	The Manifestation of the strength of Truth and Dharma.
290:	Bhootabhavya : bhavannath	The Lord the past, present and future of all beings.
291:	Pavanh:	Moving like fast wind.
292:	Pāvanah:	Purifying by His very look.
293:	Analah:	(In the form of) Fire.
294:	Kāmha:	Destroyer of the sense of doership in his devotes.
295:	Kāmkrita:	Granter of His devotees wishes.
296:	Kantah:	Extremely beautiful.
297:	Kāma:	The Trinity (with 'ka' representing Brahma,'a'representing Vishnu and 'ma' representing Mahadeva or Shiv).
298:	Kāmpradah:	Bestower to his devotees their desired objects.
299:	Prabhu:	Omnipotent Almighty.
300:	Yugādikrita:	Harbinger of the beginning of an epoch.
301:	Yugāvarta:	He who rotates all the four yugas in order like His Chakra (discus).
302:	Naikamaya:	Creator of Many Illusions.
303:	Mahāshana:	He who devours everything at the end of an epoch.

304: Adrishya:	Invisible (for those infatuated with sensual objects).
305: Vyaktaroopa:	Manifest for (of Divinity).
306: Sahastrajit:	Vanquisher of a thousand foes.
307: Anantajit:	Vanquisher of a thousand foes.
308: Ishta:	The Chosen Divinity.
309: Avishishta:	The best even without any description of the qualities.
310: Shishteshtah:	The Chosen God of the noble.
311: Shikhandi:	Making peacock feather His head ornament (in the Krishna form).
312: Nahushah:	Who enchants the mortals by his illusions.
313: Vrasha:	He who fulfils all desires.
314: Krodhahā:	Destroyer of the anger.
315: Krodhakritkarta:	Showing His wrath upon the wicked to reform them.
316: Vishwabāhu:	Having arms in every direction.
317: Maheedharah:	The support of the World.
318: Achyuta:	Free from all the six vile feelings.
319: Prathitah:	Initiator of the process of creaton.
320: Prāna:	The Vital force.
321: Prānadah:	Bestower of life.
322: Vāsavānujah:	Younger brother of Indra.
323: Apānnidhi:	A deep pit like ocean to collect water.
324: Adhishthānam:	The very support of all mortal beings.
325: Apramātah:	Not stingy in granting due reward to his devotee.
326: Pratishthita:	Well established in His Own Glory.
327: Skanda:	Commander of the gods, forces (in this form).
328: Skandadharah:	Upholder of righteousness.
329: Dhurya:	The axis of all movement in the world.
330: Varadah:	Bestower of the desired boon.
331: Vayuvāhan:	The carrier of the wind.
332: Vāsudeva:	The Abode of a all beings.
333: Vrihadbhnu:	The Mighty sun.
334: Ādideva:	Primal Deity.
335: Purandar:	Destroyer of the Cities of demons.
336: Ashoka:	One who rids all of sorrow.
337: Tāran:	One who takes across (the ocean of mundane existence).

338:	Tarah:	Who destroys the fright for death and decay.
339:	Shoor:	Valiant.
340:	Shauri:	Son of chivalrous Vasudeva (In Krishna's form).
341:	Janeshwar:	Lord of all beings.
342:	Anukool:	Towards our side.
343:	Shātāvartā:	Coming in hundred rotations (i.e.incarnating many times to protect Dharma).
344:	Padmi:	Wielder of lotus in his hand.
345:	Padmanibhekshan:	Having a sight as soft as the stalk of lotus.
346:	Padmanābha:	Having a lotus in whose navel region.
347:	Arvindākasha:	Having lotus like eyes.
348:	Padmagarbha:	Worth concentrating in the lotus of heart.
349:	Shareerabhrita:	Nourishing everybody with food.
350:	Mahardhi:	Having great glory.
351:	Riddha:	Exclling in all match.
352:	Vriddhātma:	The ancient soul.
353:	Mahāksha:	The Wide Eyed.
354:	Garudadhwajā:	He who has Garuda Mark in His Flag.
355:	Atul:	Incomparable.
356:	Sharabh:	Illumining bodies in orderly manner.
357:	Bheema:	Terrible.
358:	Samayagya:	The even reward of all the sacrifices.
359:	Havirharih:	The Reminder of His share in the Yagya offering and destroyer of sins.
360:	Sarvalakshan : lakshanya	Having all comely features.
361:	Lagahmivān:	Ever with riches (or Goddess Lakshmi).
362:	Samitinjayah	Victor in every war.
363:	Vikshar:	Decayless
364:	Rohit:	Incarnating in the form of the fish.
365:	Margah:	The path to Salvation.
366:	Hetu:	The purpose of the world.
367:	Damodar:	He whose stomach was tied with a rope (By Yashoda in his Krishna incarnation).
368:	Sah:	Tolerating every affliction for the benefit of his devotees.
369:	Maheedhar:	The Support of the world.
370:	Mahābhāg:	Supremely fortunate.

371: Vegavān:	Very fast moving.
372: Amitāshan:	One who devours the world.
373: Udbhava:	The cause of world's growth or emergence.
374: Kshobhan:	One who agitates Being and Nature before Creation.
375: Deva:	The Deity.
376: Shree garbha:	Preserving every wealth of world inside His stomach.(at the time fo Dissolution).
377: Parmeshwarah:	Supreme Lord, Almighty.
378: Kāranam:	The greatest means of creation.
379: Karanam:	The Prime Cause of World's existence.
380: Karta:	One who is totally free to act.
381: Vikarta:	The special Creator of the realms.
382: Gahan:	Intense and Mysterious.
383: Guhah:	Covering Himself with His Illusive Veil.
384: Vyavasāya:	The very source of Knowledge.
385: Vyavasthān:	One who ordains order in the Creation.
386: Sansthan:	The Abode of Dissolution.
387: Sthānadah:	He Who Granted Firm position (to His Devotees liks Dhruva and Prahlaad).
388: Dhruva:	Indestructible.
389: Parardhi:	One with Great Glory.
390: Paramspashta:	Crystal clear(before his know-ledgeable and discerning devotees).
391: Tushta:	Fully Satiate(God).
392: Pushta:	Fully Healthy.
393: Shubhekshana:	He who ensures welfare merely by His Darshan.
394: Rām:	One Who is Instinct in every bit of Creation.
395: Virām:	The final Resting Place of all beings.
396: Virat:	Indifferent (totally devoid of passion and dullness).
397: Marg:	The ultimate Path of Salvation.
398: Neyah:	Comprehensible by superior Knowledge.
399: Nayah:	The controlling and regulating factor of the world order.
400: Anayah:	Totally free, liberated.
401: Veer:	Brave.
402: Shaktimatan Shreshta:	Mightier than the mightiest.

403: Dharmah:	The Dharma or the conduct of living.
404: Dharma Viduttam:	He who knows the Dharma best.
405: Vaikuntha:	The final Abode of all aspirants.
406: Purusha:	The Primal Person.
407: Prān:	The Vital air.
408: Prānad:	The Giver of Life.
409: Pranav:	The Special form of the Monosyllable 'Om'.
410: Prathu:	Spreading in large billows.
411: Hiranyagarbha:	Holding (in His belly) the Golden Ovam.
412: Shatrughna:	The Slayer of the enemies.
413: Vyāpta:	All round spreading.
414: Vāyu:	The Vital air.
415: Adhokshaja:	Of undecayable form.
416: Ritu:	Visible by the cycle fo time (the seasons).
417: Sudershan:	Having auspicious appearance; good to look at.
418: Kaal:	The Measure of All.
419: Parameshthee:	Excelling in His great glory.
420: Parigriha:	Approachable form all sides by the shelter seekers.
421: Ugra:	The Wrathful, causing fear even in the fire and son gods.
422: Sanvatsarah:	The Beginner of the cycle.
423: Daksha:	Dextrous in all works.
424: Vishrām:	The final Resting Place of all the seekers of Moksha.
425: Vishwadakshin:	The receiver of all 'Dakshina' in the sacrifice arranged by Bali.
426: Vistar:	The cause of expansion of the Universe.
427: Sthāvarathānu:	Though Himself stable yet keeping the world amove.
428: Pramānam:	The ultimate evidence of existence of world.
429: Beejamavyam:	The Imperishable Entity of the world.
430: Artha:	Adorable by all owing to His being bestower of happiness.
431: Anartha:	Having no desire, so it is meaningless to offer Him anything.
432: Māhākoshā:	One with Great Treasure.
433: Mahabhoga:	The Great Enjoyer.
434: Mahadhana:	Supremely and Really Rich.

435: Anirviana:	Free form the surfeit or boredom.
436: Sthavishtha:	Reposing Everywhere.
437: Abhoo:	Unborn.
438: Dharma Yoop:	The pillar of Dharma.
439: Mahāmakha:	Making great a sacrifice (in which offering is made to Him).
440: Nakshatranemi:	The Centre of all planet and constellations.
441: Nakshatri:	Moon-like.
442: Kshamah:	Competent.
443: Kshāmah:	Capable of quelling all disorders.
444: Sameehanah:	Making conscious efforts for creation.
445: Yagya:	Embodiment of all sacrifices.
446: Ijyah:	Adorable.
447: Mahejyah:	Most Adorable (among all deities).
448: Kratuh:	Lord of the Sacrifice with all the appurtneances.
449: Satram:	Protector of the noble.
450: Satam Gatih:	The ultimate destination of the nobles.
451: Sarvadarshee:	One who looks at all.
452: Vimuktakāmā:	Free form the mortal desires.
453: Sarvagya:	All knowing.
454: Gyanmuttamam:	The Best Knowledge.
455: Suvratah:	Of noble resolve.
456: Sumukhah:	Of beautiful visage.
457: Sukhadah:	Bestower of happiness to His devotee.
458: Sukshmah:	Very Subtle.
459: Sughoshah:	Having a sweet and deep voice.
460: Suhrita:	Kind to all being without any selfish desire.
461: Manohar:	Enchanting.
462: Jitakrodha:	He who has subdued his anger.
463: Veerbāhu:	Mighty Armed.
464: Vidaranah:	Tearing apart the wicked.
465: Swapan:	He who throws everyone in the stupor during the Dissolution (Pralaya).
466: Swavash:	Self-Dependent.
467: Vyāpi:	All pervading.
468: Naikatmā:	Adpiting various forms in every age according to the need of time.
469: Naikakarmakrita:	Indulging in varous activities (like

creation, destruction etc.) for people's welfare.

470: Vatsar: Ultimate Abode of All.

471: Vatsal: Very Affectionate to His devotees.

472: Vatsy: Rearing up the heifer (in Vrindavan as Krishna).

473: Ratnagarbh: Hiding gems inside his person.

474: Dhaneshwar: Lord of all riches.

475: Dharmgup: The Protector of Dharma.

476: Dharmakrita: Showing by action how to uphold the righteousness.

477: Dharmi: The base of all Dharmic tenets.

478: Sat: True (Being).

479: Asat: The False worldly form.

480: Ksharam: Causing decay in physical entities or the Decadent.

481: Aksaharam: Making (things) Imperishable.

482: Avigyātā: Soul in the body is called 'Vigyātā. That which is distinct from it-the supreme spirt-or Lord Vishnu-is Avigyātā.

483: Sahastrānshu: Like a sun with thousand rays.

484: Vidhātā: The special carrier of the whole world.

485: Kritalakshan: Anointed with noble signs like 'Shree Vatsa'.

486: Gabhastinemi: Reposed like the sun among the rays.

487: Satvastha: Omnipresent; knowing truth of every heart.

488: Sinha: Adopting the Lion (visage) for Prahlaad's cause.

489: Bhootamaheshwar: Lord of all mortal creation.

490: Ādideva: The Primal Deity.

491: Mahadeva: The Grand Deity.

492: Devesha: Lord of all Deities.

493: Devbhridaguru: The Guru of the gods who takes special care of them.

494: Uttarah: The other bang of the ocean of metempsychosis.

495: Gopati: The Lord and protector of Cows (as Krishna).

496: Gopta: He who protects and nourishes every being.

497: Gyāngamya: Comprehensible by knowledge.

498: Purātān:	The Ancient Being.
499: Shareerabhootbhrita:	The nourisher of the five basic elements of the body.
500: Bhokta:	The one who Enjoys Eternal Bliss.
501: Kapeendra:	Lord of Monkeys (or King of Monkeys, Shri Rām).
502: Bhooridakshina:	One Who gives fees to the priests liberally.
503: Somepah:	The Partaker of 'Soma' offered to Him in the yagyas.
504: Amritapah:	He who drings nectar and makes other gods also drink ti.
505: Soma:	The moon who nourishes all vegetables.
506: Purujit:	Victorious of many battles.
507: Purusattam:	The Best Universal form.
508: Vinaya:	The Punisher of the Wicked.
509: Jaya:	The Victor (or the cause of victory).
510: Satyasandha:	Veridicious.
511: Dashārha:	Appearing in the Dashārha family.
512: Satvatām Pati:	The Leader of Yadavas and the Lord of his devotees.
513: Jeeva:	The Being.
514: Vinayitāsākshi:	He who discerns the humility of his devotees quickly.
515: Mukundah:	The Bestower of Liberation.
516: Amitavikramah:	Immensely competent to bring Revolution.
517: Ambhonidhi:	Huge like sea, the store of water.
518: Anantātmā:	The Soul Infinite.
519: Mahodadhishaya:	He who Reposes in the Grand Ocean even during Pralay-time, agitation and disturbance.
520: Antakah:	Death like to end being's life (at Pralaya).
521: Ajaha:	Free form blemish of getting birth.
522: Maharhah:	Adorable.
523: Swābhāvya:	Owing to the self-evidence of the Existence, the need of whose birth does not arise.
524: Jitamitrah:	Friend of the wicked's enemies (the gods).
525: Pramodanah:	He who Delights merely by remembering Him.

526: Ānada:	Bliss {or the Manifestation of Bliss}.
527: Nandanah:	The Delighter of all.
528: Nandah:	Prosperous with all comforts and luxuries.
529: Satyadhrma:	The Truth of the faith.
530: Trivikram:	Measuring three realms in His three steps. (Vāman).
531: Maharshi: Kapilācharya	The Propounder of the Sankhya Theory (the sage Kapil).
532: Kritagya:	Grateful (to his devotees for the devotion).
533: Medanipati:	The Lord of Earth.
534: Tripadah:	He Who measured all the realms in three steps.
535: Tridashādhyaksha:	Lord of all gods, demons and men.
536: Mahashringah:	He Who Has a Great Thorn (as the Boar).
537: Kritāntakrita:	He Who Removes the need of the deed when invoked {i.e., He ilberates when worshipped}.
538: Mahāvārah:	The Great Boar.{The Second Incarnation}.
559: Govindah:	He Who is Capable of Reclaiming the sunken earth.
540: Sushenah:	Well attended by an army of lieutenants.
541: Kanakāngadi:	He Who Has a golden armlet.
542: Guhyah:	The Occult {Who occultly resides in every heart}.
543: Gabheerah:	Of very deep nature.
544: Gahan:	Very Intense.
545: Guptah:	Secret, incomprehensible by description.
546: Chakragadadharam:	The Weilder of the Disc and the Mace.
547: Vedhah:	One Who Constitutes Everything.
548: Swāngah:	Self-supporting.
549: Ajitah:	Invincible.
550: Krishnah:	Lord ShriKrishna.
551: Dridhah:	Determined.
552: Sankarshanoachhyut:	Infallible by any attraction.
553: Varuna:	The Lord of Waters.
554: Vārunah:	The son of Lord of waters, varuna-or Vashishth.

555: Vriksha:	The Tree of Ashwattha (The Peepal Tree).
556: Pushkarāksha:	The Lotus Eyed.
557: Mahāmanah:	He Who accomplishes anything by merely thinking about it.
558: Bhagwan:	The God having all the six divine Attributes.
559: Bhagha:	He Who withdraws all opulence of his devotees in order to test the firmess of their devotion.
560: Ānandi	He Who is Manifestation of Bliss.
561: Vanmāli:	He Who Has a garland of wild flowers-Vaijayanti.
562: Halāyudh:	The Plough-Holder (Balrām).
563: Āditya:	Son of Aditi.
564: Jyotirāditya:	The Brilliant Sun.
565: Sahishnu:	Capable of bearing all the opposites'effect simultaneously.
566: Gatisattam:	The noble's destination.
567: Sudhanvā:	Weilder of a beautiful bow.
568: Khanda Parashu:	In the form of Parashurām, the Axe Holder.
569: Dārunah:	Terrible (For those treading unrighteous path).
570: Dravinapradah:	The Bestower of riches to His devotes who want them.
571: Divasprik:	Spreading upto heaven.
572: Savradrigvyās:	The All Seeing Vyas (Vedavyas)
573: Vāchaspatiryonijah:	Master of Knowledge and not born thorugh the vagina (i.e; Self created).
574: Trisāmā:	Whose glory is sung by the three Vedas.
575: Samagah:	He who sings Sām Veda.
576: Nirvānam:	The Abode of the Liberated Soul.
577: Sām:	Embodiment of Sām Veda.
578: Bheshajam:	The Medicine for Mortal ills.
579: Bhishak:	The ultimate Physician to cure all ills.
580: Sanyās-krita:	He who Ordained Sanyas-Ashram for the aspirant desiring salvation.
581: Shamah:	The Queller (of the disturbance caused by the wicked).
582: Shantih:	Embodiment of Quietude.

583:	Nishtha:	The Object of everybody's loyalty.
584:	Shantih:	Peace personified.
585:	Parayanam:	The final Abode of the Salvation seekers.
586:	Shubhāngah:	He Who has Beautiful organs and Body.
587:	Shantidah:	He Who Gives peace.
588:	Srashta:	The Creator.
589:	Kumudah:	The Delighter of the Earth.
590:	Kuvaleshaya:	He Who Reposes on the Serpent's coil in water.
591:	Gohitah:	The well-wisher of cows.
592:	Gopati:	Lord of cows.
593:	Gopta:	Keeping Himself Enveloped by His Creative Illusion.
594:	Vrishabhāksha:	Having Gracious look for all.
595:	Vrishabha-priya:	The Lover of Dharma.
596:	Anivarti:	The Lover of Dharma.
597:	Nivrarti:	Indomitable in War or in the protection of Dharma.
598:	Samksheptā:	He Who Condenses the World in a trice.
599:	Kshemkrita:	The protector of the shelter-seekers.
600:	Shiv:	The Auspicious.
601:	Sreevatsavaksha:	Having 'Shree vatsa' mark upon His Bosom.
602:	Shreevāsah:	The Abode of Lakshmi.
603:	Shreepati:	Lord of Lakshmi.
604:	Shreematam Varah:	The Best Groom.
605:	Shreedah:	Giver of all wealth.
606:	Shreesha:	Lord of Lakshmi.
607:	Shreeniwas:	Abode of Lakshmi.
608:	Shreenidhi:	Fount of all wealth.
609:	Shreevibhavan:	Granter of the desired fruit according to devotees' efforts.
610:	Shreedhara:	He in whose bosom reposes Lakshmi.
611:	Shreekarah:	He Who Gives all opulence and peace to His devotees.
612:	Shreyah:	Auspiciousess personified.
613:	Shreemān:	Having all sorts of riches.
614:	Lokatryashrāya:	The Support for all the three Realms.
615:	Swaksha:	Having Beautiful Eyes.
616:	Swangah:	Having Beautiful organs.
617:	Shatānanda:	Bestower of a Hundred Kinds of Happiness and Bliss.

618:	Nandi:	Image of the Supreme Bliss.
619:	Jyotirganeshwar˙	Lord of all luminaries.
620:	Vijitatmā:	He Who Has His Mind under His Control.
621:	Avidheyatmā:	Whose real Form is ineffable.
622:	Satkirtee:	One with Real Glory.
623:	Chinnasamshaya:	He Who Removes All Doubts.
624:	Udeerna:	Best Among all Beings.
625:	Sarvatashchakshu:	He who can see everything in all directions at all times.
626:	Aneesha:	Having no one Above Him.
627:	Shāshwatasthira:	Eternal and immutable.
628:	Bhooshayah:	He Who slept on the Earth (in the form of Rām).
629:	Bhooshanah:	An ornament (of the earth by his incarnations).
630:	Bhootih:	The Support of all Existences.
631:	Vishokah:	Free from all woes.
632:	Shokanāshanah:	Destroyer of sorrow.
633:	Archishmān:	The Source of brightness of all luminaries.
634:	Architah:	Worshipped by all.
635:	Kumbha:	The Pitcher (of existence).
636:	Vishuddhātmā:	Pure Soul.
637:	Vishodhanah:	He who purifies All.
638:	Aniruddha:	Unstoppable.
639:	Apratirath:	Having no oppisition.
640:	Pradyumna:	Indomitable to His adversary.
641:	Amitavikrama:	Of Infinite valour.
642:	Kalinemihā:	The slayer of the demon Kalinemi.
643:	Veer:	Chivalrous.
644:	Shauri:	Born in the family of the gallant (Shree Krishna).
645:	Shoorjaneshwar:	The Chosen Lord, owing to His powers, for Indra and other gods.
646:	Trilokātamā:	The Spirit pervading the Three Realms.
647:	Trilokesha:	The Lord of the Three Realms.
648:	Keshavah:	Having hair as shiny as the rays of the sun.
649:	Keshihā:	Slayer of Keshi.
650:	Hari:	He whose mere rememberance causes all sins and affictions to disappear.

651: Kāmdeva:	The Deity who fulfils all desires.
652: Kāmpal:	Satiator of all desires.
653: Kāmi:	He whose desires are ever fulfilled.
654: Kantah:	Very Enchanting person.
655: Kritagamah:	Author of all scriptures.
656: Anirdeshyavapu:	Whose Divine form is ineffable.
657: Vishnu:	The Lord (of the Trinity who preserves the world).
658: Veerah:	Who treads even without moving his feet and having many divine powers.
659: Anantah:	Infinite.
660: Dhananjaya:	Winner of wealth.
661: Brahmanya:	Protector of the Brahman, the noble and of knowledge.
662: Brahmakrita:	Who created order for Brahmans.
663: Brahma:	In the form of Brahmā, the creator.
664: Brahm:	Supreme spirit.
665: Brahmvivardhanah:	Enhancer of the Brahm (or its Manifestation).
666: Brahmavit:	Knower of the Meaning of the Vedas fully.
667: Brahmanah:	Looking at all without prejudice or prediliction.
668: Brahmi:	The Divine spirit permeating all.
669: Brahmagya:	He who knows Brahm (and scriptures etc).
670: Brahmanpriya:	Darling of Brahmans.
671: Mahākrama:	Perfomer of great feats.
672: Mahākarma:	Perfomer of great deeds.
673: Mahātejah:	The Radiance of the Radiant.
674: Mahoraga:	The Great Serpent (Vāsuki).
675: Mahākratu:	Embodiment of a Great Sacrifice.
676: Mahāyajwa:	He Who Performs Great Sacrifice for peoples' welfare.
677: Māhāyagya:	A Great yagya(Deed or Action).
678: Mahāhavi:	The Great offering.
679: Stavya:	Adorable for every one.
680: Stavapriya:	He who gets propitiated by chanting hymns.
681: Strotram:	The Hymn (For singing Lord's glory).
682: Stuti:	The obtect of orisons.
683: Ranapriya:	He Who loves wars.

684:	Poornah:	Perfect in every way.
685:	Stota:	He Who creates hymns.
686:	Pooriyata:	He Who makes His devotee devoid of want.
687:	Punya:	The Spirit behind a meritorious deed.
688:	Punyakeerti:	Of noble renown.
689:	Anāmayah:	Free from any kind of affliction.
690:	Manotava:	Traveller with the speed of mind.
691:	Teerthakarah:	Creator of All Knowledege and Its Interpreter.
692:	Vasuretā:	The Seed of Existence.
693:	Vasupradah:	Bestower of all riches.
694:	Vāsudeva:	Son of Vasudeva (Shree Krishna).
695:	Vāsuprad:	Bestower of Great Wealth in the form of Moksha (or final release).
696:	Vasu:	The Abode of All Beings.
697:	Vasumana:	The Dweller in All Hearts.
698:	Havi:	The Supreme offering (of the Yagya).
699:	Sadgati:	The Final Stage of the noble.
700:	Satkriti:	The (Performer of the) Noble Deed (to perserve the world).
701:	Sattā:	The Authority
702:	Sadbhooti:	Visible in many Forms.
703:	Satpāryān:	The Desired Destination of the noble.
704:	Shoorsena:	The Commander of the army of Valiants (in His Rām Incarnation, Having Hanumān, Jambvant and others).
705:	Yadushrestha:	The Best among the family of Yadu (as Krishna).
706:	Sannivās:	The Abode of the noble.
707:	Suyāmunah:	Whose Presence conesecrated the river Yamuna bank. (Shree Krishnu).
708:	Bhootavās:	The ultimate Abode of all mortals.
709:	Vāsudeva:	The Deity who Envelops the world by His Illusion.
710:	Sarvāsunilaya:	The Besutiful Home for the noble.
711:	Analah:	Endowed with Immense power and wealth.
712:	Darpahā:	Browbeater of the arrogant.
713:	Driptah:	Immersed in the Eternal Bliss.
714:	Durdharah:	Difficul place in heart.
715:	Darpadah:	Bestower of the glory to His devotees.

716: Aparājita:	Invincible.
717: Vishwamoorti:	The Form Universal.
718: Mahamoorti:	Of the Grand Image.
719: Deeptimoorti:	Having radiant Image.
720: Amoortimān:	He Whose Image Can't be Defined.
721: Anekamoorti:	Having Myriad Images.
722: Avyaktā:	Unmanifest.
723: Shatmoorti:	Having hundreds of Images.
724: Shatānanah:	Having hundred of faces.
725: Ekah:	Unique.
726: Naikah:	Owing to Many Forms, He is multi-Faceted.
727: Savah:	The Receptacle which holds the sap of the herb soma.
728: Kah:	The Embodiment of Bliss.
729: Kim:	Who Is He-the question.
730: Yat:	Self-Evident.
731: Tat:	The Expander.
732: Padamanuttamam:	The Highest State (aspired by the nobles).
734: Lokanath:	Master of the people.
735: Madhavah:	Born in Madhu's family.
736: Bhaktavatsal:	Kind to His Devotees.
737: Suvarnavarna:	Having Aureate Body Hue.
738: Hemāng:	Having Golden Body (or organs)
739: Varānga:	Having an Exalted physique.
740: Chandanāngadi:	Having His Body anointed with sandal paste.
741: Veeraha:	Slayer of demons for protecting Dharma.
742: Visham:	The only One (Having none like Him).
743: Shoonya:	Beyond all definitons.
744: Dhritāshi:	Resolute with Soft Kindness to His votaries.
745: Achala:	Unmoving (Form His Resolve).
746: Chala:	Moveable (like wind everywhere).
747: Amāni:	Not Caring For His Individual Honour.
748: Manadah:	Bestowing honour (to His devotees).
749: Lokaswami:	Master of all realms.
750: Manya:	Respectable for everyone.
751: Trilokdhrik:	The Lone Support for the Three worlds (heaven, earth and patal).

752: Sumedha:	Having Noble Brilliance.
753: Medhajah:	He who Manlests Himself though Yagya.
754: Dhanya:	The Blessed Lord.
755: Satyamedhā:	Having only Truth carying wisdom.
756: Dharādhar:	The Support of the Earth.
757: Tejovrasha:	He who Showers Brilliance upon His Devotees.
758: Dyutidhar:	Bedight with a Dazzling Brilliance.
759: Sarvashastrabhritām: Narah	The Best Among all the weapon weilders.
760: Pragraha:	He who Accepts offerings of His Devotees.
761: Nigraha:	All Restraint Personified.
762: Vyagrah:	Restless to Fulfil His devotees desires.
763: Naikashringa:	Having many media for His Resounding word.
764: Gadāgrajah:	Elder to Gada.
765: Chaturmoorti:	The Four Visaged Image.
766: Chaturbahu:	Having four Arms.
767: Chaturvyooha:	Encircled by the four arrays (Generations). 3. Four generations are represented by Vāsudeva, Sankarshan (Balram), Pradyumna and Aniruddha).
768: Chaturgatih:	Manifesting in four forms (Rām, Bharat, Lakshman, Shatrughna).
769: Chaturātmā:	Having four forms of consciouness (Mind, Wisdom, the sense of I'ness and heart).
770: Chaturbhāvah:	The origin of Four wants of the body (Dharma, Artha, Kām, Moksha).
771: Chaturvedavita:	He Who knows the Real Meaning of the four vedas.
772: Ekapat:	He Who Measured the World by His One step.
773: Samāvartā:	He Who Keeps the World Moving with even pace.
774: Nrivattatma:	The Relaxed Soul.
775: Durjaya:	Difficult to subdue.
776: Duratikrama:	He whose order is inviolable.
777: Durlabha:	Rare to perceive.
778: Durgama:	Inaccessible.
779: Durgah:	Difficult to reach.

780:	Durāvas:	Difficult to hold (in one's heart).
781:	Durārihā:	Slayer of the Demons who tread the unrighteous path.
782:	Shubhangah:	Having Beautiful Body.
783:	Lokasāranga:	He who's the Essence of the world.
784:	Sutāntu:	Having beautiful bond to bind the world in one body.
785:	Tantuvardhan:	The Enricher of the Mortal Bonds.
786:	Indrakarmā:	Performing Indra-like Deeds.
787:	Mahākarmā:	Performer of Great Deeds.
788:	Kritakarmā:	He Who Has Done All that was Due.
789:	Krtitāgam:	The Creator of the Vedas.
790:	Udbhava:	Incarnating Himself at Will.
791:	Sundarah:	Beautiful.
792:	Sundah:	Extremely kind.
793:	Ratnanābh:	Having Navel As Beautiful as a gem.
794:	Sulochana:	Of Beautiful Eyes.
795:	Arkah:	Adorable by the adored.
796:	Vājasanah:	Bestower of Food to the Hungry.
797:	Shringi:	Having a Thorn (in his Fish Incannation)
798:	Jayantah:	The Victor of the enemy.
999:	Sarvavijjayee:	Victor All.
800:	Suvarnabindu:	Having Golden pointed Name. 4. In Nagari script, it is written ॐ (the point represents god)] (the word OM).
801:	Akshobhya:	He who cannot be Disturbed or agitated.
802:	Sarvāgeeshwar eshwar:	The Lord of all Sounds.
803:	Mahahrida:	The Great pond (of Bliss for the Yogis).
804:	Mahagarta:	The Grand Entity (Undecayed even in the pralaya).
805:	Mahabhoota:	The Grand Entity (Undecayed even in the pralaya).
806:	Mahanidhi:	The Grand Abode of All.
807:	Kumudah:	Redeemer of the Earth ('Ku')'s burden.
808:	Kundarah:	Penetrator of the Earth (to kill Hiranyakshapa)
809:	Kundah:	The Donor of the Earth (to sage Kashyapa).
810:	Purjanya:	He who showers All Desired Objects.
811:	Pāvan:	Purifier.
812:	Anilah	Ever Awake.
813:	Amritānsh:	He whose Hope is Never Belied.

814: Amritavapu: Of Imperishable Body.
815: Sarvagya: Omniscient.
816: Sarvatomukh: Having Face in Every Direction.
817: Sulabha: Easily Accessible (to the devotee).
818: Suvratah: He who Eats Good Food (offered by His devotees).
819: Siddhah: Endowed with perfection
820: Shatrujita: Vanquisher of the Enemy.
821: Shatrutapān: Scorcher of the Foe.
822: Nyagrodha: The Grand Banyan.
823: Udambar: He who stays Beyond the skies.
824: Chānoorāndhranishoodan: He who killed the Werstler of Andhra tribe, Chānoora.
825: Ashwatth: The Peepal (tree-believed to be most pious).
826: Sahastrārchi: Having Infinite Rays.
827: Saptajivha: The Seven Tongued Flame.
828: Saptadha: The Fire with Seven Radiances.
829: Saptavāhan: The Sun Having vehicle with Seven Horses.
830: Amoortih: Formless.
831: Anagha: Free from all sins.
832: Bhayakrita: Frightening (to the wicked).
833: Achintya: Beyond Comprehension.
834: Bhayanashan: Destroyer of the fright (for his devotees).
835: Anuh: The Molecule.
836: Vribhatah: Huge.
837: Krishah: Very light and thin.
838: Sthoola: The Heavy (Huge)Bodied.
839: Gunabhrita: The Mine of All virtues.
840: Nirgunah: The Attributeless.
841: Mahān: The Great.
842: Adhrita: Whom no one could carry (or possess).
843: Swadhritā: Self-Carrier.
844: Swasya: Of Beautiful Visage.
845: Pragvansha: The Origin of all families.
846: Vanshavardhan: He who Augments Families.
847: Bhārbhritā: The Carrier of (the Earth's) load.
848: Kathīlā: Repeatedly described (by the scriptures).
849: Yogi: Ever in communion (with his world).
850: Yogesha: Lord of all yogis.
851: Sarvākāmad: Fulfiller of all desires.

852: Aashramah:	The Resting place for all.
853: Shraman:	The Scourge of the wicked.
854: Kshāmah:	The Queller of Every Being During the Dissolution.
855: Suparnah:	In the Form of Garuda with beautiful wings.
856: Vayuvāhan:	He who Imparts wind the capacity to move.
857: Dhanurdharah:	The Bow Weilder (Shree Rām).
858: Dhanurvedah:	An Expert in Archery.
859: Dandah:	The Staff for punishment of the wicked.
860: Damayita:	The Ruler (like Yama) to keep vile forces in control.
861: Damah:	Reforming the wicked by adequate punishment.
862: Aparājitah:	Never Defeated.
863: Sarvasaha:	Having capacity to tolerate everything.
864: Niyantā:	He who Defines every being's duty.
865: Aniyam:	Unbound by any regulation.
866: Ayamah:	Beyond the limti to Death or any bondage.
867: Satvavāna:	Having all puissance.
868: Sattvik:	Of Noble Demeanour.
869: Satya:	The Truth.
870: Satyadharmap: ārāyanah	He who Adheres to the Righteous path, the Dharma, truthfully.
871: Abhiprāyah:	The Ultimate Meaning.
872: Priyārha:	He who Deserves to be offered one's dearest object or thing.
873: Priyakrita	He Who Does What is Good (for his devotees).
874: Arhah:	Supremely Adorable for all.
875: Preetivardhan:	He who Enriches affection for Him in His Dearest votaries.
876: Vihāyasagatih:	He who Moves in the Skies.
877: Jyotih:	The Supreme Radiance.
878: Suruchih:	Having comely grace and choicest taste.
879: Hitabhuk:	He who Accepts the Offerings made in a sacrifice.
880: Vibhuh:	All Pervading.
881: Ravi:	The Usurper of All Sap of the Creation, the Sun.

882: Virochan:	He Who Spreads Light in All Directions.
883: Surya:	He who unveils the pulchri-tude;the Sun.
884: Savitā:	The Begetter of the Entire universe.
885: Ravilochana:	He who has the Sun as His eye.
886: Anantah:	He who is Endless.
887: Hutabhuk:	The Consumer of All offerings.
888: Bhokta:	The Enjoyer of All Natural Bounties.
889: Sukhadah:	The Bestower of Happiness (to his devotee).
890: Narkajah:	Having Infinite Births for the protection of the noble and Dharma.
891: Agrajah:	The First Born;The Primal Being.
892: Anirvannah:	He who is Never Bored (by any activity).
893: Sadāmarshee:	He who Ever Forgives the noble.
894: Lokadhishthanam:	The Prop of the Entire Realms.
895: Adbhutah:	Amazing.
896: Sanāt:	The Form At the Final Hour.
897: Sanātantamah:	The Cause and Root of All; the Oldest Being.
898: Kapilah:	The sage Kapil.
899: Kepih:	The Sun-god.
900: Apyaha	The point of Final coalescence.
901: Swastidah::	He who Ensures Welfare of All.
902: Swastikritah:	The Auspicious Refuge of the noblce.
903: Swasti:	The Embodiment of All that is Auspicious.
904: Swastibhuk:	He who protects welfare of His devotees.
905: Swastidakshinah:	The Right Hand Ensuring Welfare to His devotees.
906: Araudra:	The Embodiment of peace sans all wrath.
907: Kundali:	The wearer of the (corcodile shaped) Ear-rings as bright as the sun.
908: Chakri:	The Weilder of the Discus Sudarshan.
909: Vikrami:	He who Sits In Revolution.
910: Uoorjitashāsan:	Whose Adminstration, as Ordained through the Scriptures, is the Best.
911: Shabdātigah:	He who is Beyond the range of Voice or Sound.
912: Shabdasah:	He whose glory is Described by the Scriptures.
913: Shishirah:	The Cool Image for those afflicted by the Oppressive heat of three kinds (the

	physical, the mental and the spiritual).
914: Sharvarikarah:	He who is Night of Enlightenment for the learned and Night of Ignorance for the ignorants -i.e. He who Creates both sorts of Night Himself.
915: Akroora:	He who has no feeling of Cruelty.
916: Peshalah:	Supremely Beautiful Owing to his auspicious voice, mind and deeds.
917: Dakshah:	The Expert or Efficient (in every art).
918: Dakshinah:	The Destroyer.
919: Kshaminam Varah:	Best Among those who Forgives.
920: Vidwattamah:	The Most Learned Scholar.
921: Veetabhayah:	Free from all fright.
922: Punyashravan keertan:	He listening to whose glories and singing whose hymns grant all merit.
923: Uttārana:	He who takes (the soul) across the ocean of metempsychosis.
924: Dushkritaha:	He who Destroys the sin of sinner.
925: Punya:	Whose very remembrance gives one merit.
926: Duhawapnanāshan:	The Destroyer of the Nightmares.
927: Veerahā:	He who gallantly alters the course of His devotees'Destiny.
928: Rakshanah:	He who protects the noble by all means.
929: Sant:	He who spreads educatio and humility by his action and voice.
930: Jeevanah:	The Very life of all Existence.
931: Paryavastihah:	He who pervades All world But Himself Remains Stationary.
932: Anataroop:	He who Has Infinite Forms.
933: Anantashree:	He Who Has Immense Psychic powers.
934: Jitamanyu:	He who has subdued anger.
935: Bhayāpah:	He who Removes fear from His devotees'heart.
936: Chatturashtrah:	The Embodiment of all Vedic Knowledge and Just.
937: Gabheerātma:	He who has depth in His character.
938: Vidishah:	He who gives each what is due on the basis of the deed performed.
939: Vyādishah:	He who Gives Appropriate orders to all (or who Assigns every Being's Duty).

940: Dishah:	Like the Vedas showing the right directions.
941: Anādi:	He who had no Beginning.
942: Bhoorbhuvah:	The Support of this Earth.
943: Lakshmi:	The Sheen of all beauteous objects.
944: Suveerah:	He who Inspires faith in the devotees' hearts.
945: Ruchirāngadah:	He who Dons auspicious armlets.
946: Jananah:	The Origin of All Beings.
947: Janmajanmādi:	The Root Cause of all beings' birth.
948: Bheemah:	Terrible for the wicked.
949: Bheema-parākramah:	performer of the Terrifying feats for the wicked.
950: Ādharnilaya:	The Support of the Earth and all the beings.
951: Adhāta:	He who could not be carried (created) by anyone.
952: Pushpahās:	He whose laughter is like the Blooming flower.
953: Prajāgarah:	He who is ever conscious and Awakened.
954: Uoordhvagah:	He who Dwells at the top.
955: Satpathāchar:	He who Ever Moves on the Righteous Path.
956: Prānadah:	He who Resuscitates the dead (like Pareekshitah, who was born dead, but brought to life by Lord Krishna, an Incarnation of Lord Vishnu).
957: Pranavah:	The Form of the syllable Onkar.
958: Panah:	He Whose Behaviour Is Ideal with all; Worldliwise.
959: Pramānam:	The Evidence (or Self Evident).
960: Pranānilaya:	The Basis of life.
961: Prānabrita:	The Nourisher of life.
962: Prānjeevan:	The Vital Air to keep all beings alive.
963: Tattvam:	The Essence (or the Reality).
964: Tattvavita:	He who knows the Reality.
965: Ekātma:	Unique; without A Second.
966: Janmamrityu-jarātigah:	Beyond life and death or decay or beyone mortal bondage.
967: Bhoorbhuvahs Wastaruh:	The Tree of Existence permeating all the three Realms.

968: Tarah:	He who makes one (his devotee) transcend the sea of life and death.
969: Savita:	The Grand Deity causing birth of every being; the Sun.
970: Prapitāmah:	The Sire of the Grand Deity Brahma.
971: Yagyah:	The cause of all activities the world.
972: Yagyapatih:	The Lord of all yagyas or the Decider of all activities.
973: Yajwa:	He who is also the Host of the yagya or sacrifice.
974: Yagyangah:	The Embodiment of all organs of a yagya or the One who decides every activity in a yagya.
975: Yagyavāhan:	The Moving Spirit behind every yagya-the prime Mover of every activity.
976: Yagyabhrit:	He Who Nourishes every activity.
977: Yagyakrita:	The performer of the yagya or who makes every yagya an accomplish-ment.
978: Yagyee:	The Ultimate goal of every yagya or the final outcome of every or the final outcome of every activity.
979: Yagyabhuk:	He who Enjoys the outcome of every activity.
980: Yagyasādhana:	The Deity or the Ultimate Aim for which the Yagyas are performed.
981: Yagyantakrita:	He who Ends every yagya or who Bestows the Reward of every yagya.
982: Yagyaguhyam:	The Imperceptible Manifestation of Knowledge through Yagya.
983: Annam:	The Bestower of Cereal or Food for every Being.
984: Annād:	The Eater of all food.
985: Atmayoni:	He who caused His own creation;or the Self-created.
986: Swayamjātah:	He who creates Himself at His will.
987: Vaikhānah:	The Digger of Earth {Lord Vishnu dug earth in His Boar Incarnation to slay Hiranyakashapa who dwelled inside the bowels of the earth}.
988: Sāmgayanah:	He who Chants the Hymns of Sām Veda.
989: Devakinandan:	Son of Mother Devaki (in His Shree Krishna Incarnation}.

990: Srishtā:	The procreator of All Realms; the Cause of Existnece.
991: Kshiteesha:	Master of Earth.
992: Papanāshan:	The Destroyer of Sin (merely by His remembrance and worship).
993: Shankhabhrita:	The Weilder of the conch-shell called Panchajanya.
994: Nandaki:	The Weilder of the Sword called Nandak.
995: Chakri:	The Weilder of the Discus called Sudarshan.
996: Sharngadhanva:	The Weilder of the Bow called Sharnga.
997: Gadādhar:	The Weilder of the mace called Kaumudi.
998: Rathāngpāni:	He who weilded the wheel of the chariot as his discus to challenge Bheeshma Pitamah in the Mahabharat war.
999: Askshobhya:	He who can't be frightened by anyone or anything.
1000: Sarvapraharan: āyudhah	He who is the Weilder of all those Known and nuknown weapons used in war.

Om Namo Bhagwate Vasudevaaya